79 — 81
6? — ?1
66) 63
45) 48, 49, 22, 23, 24, 31

EXERCISES
in ENGLISH

LEVEL C

LOYOLAPRESS.

CHICAGO

Consultants

Therese Elizabeth Bauer
Martina Anne Erdlen
Anita Patrick Gallagher
Patricia Healey
Irene Kervick
Susan Platt

Linguistics Advisor

Timothy G. Collins
National-Louis University

Series Design: Loyola Press
Interior Art:
Jim Mitchell: 1, 5, 15, 29, 41, 77, 84, 91.
Greg Phillips: 7, 8, 18, 24, 25, 26, 34, 66, 70, 72, 74, 80, 88, 92.
All interior illustrations not listed above are by Jean Wisenbaugh/lindgrensmith.com.

ISBN-10: 0-8294-2335-4; ISBN-13: 978-0-8294-2335-8

Exercises in English® is a registered trademark of Loyola Press.

Manufactured in the United States of America.

06 07 08 09 10 11 12 VonH 10 9 8 7 6 5 4 3 2 1

Contents

DIAGRAMMING

Name _____

1. Sentences

> A **sentence** is a group of words that expresses a complete thought. Every sentence has a subject (a person, a place, a thing, or an idea) and a predicate (an action or a state of being).
>
> | SUBJECT | PREDICATE |
> |---|---|
> | George Washington and his wife | lived at Mount Vernon. |
> | His wife's name | was Martha. |

Read each example. Write **S** on the line if the words form a sentence. Put a period at the end of each sentence.

_____ 1. George Washington had a large farm in Virginia

_____ 2. Tobacco and wheat

_____ 3. Washington raised horses and cattle

_____ 4. Once he even owned a buffalo

_____ 5. The farm had a flour mill and a blacksmith shop

_____ 6. Workers on the farm made cloth, shoes, and barrels

_____ 7. A peach and an apple orchard

_____ 8. Some supplies had to be ordered from England

_____ 9. Farm implements, tools, paint, hats, and silk stockings

_____ 10. "Buy nothing you can make yourselves," Washington said

George Washington believed in being self-sufficient. Give examples of things you are able to do without help from others.

2. Statements and Questions

Telling sentences are called **statements**.
A statement ends with a period.

> **George Washington owned a large farm.**

Asking sentences are called **questions**.
A question ends with a question mark.

> **Do you know the name of his farm?**

Every sentence begins with a capital letter.

A. Put a period at the end of each statement and a question mark at the end of each question.

1. Have you ever been on a farm

2. There are many jobs to do on a farm

3. Everybody in the family helps

4. What kinds of jobs do farmers do

5. Some farmers grow fruits, vegetables, or grains

6. Farmers have to water their crops

7. Other farmers raise animals

8. Farm children help to feed the animals

9. Do you think it is harder to raise crops or animals

10. Why is a farmer's work important

B. Make statements and questions by matching the words in Column A with the words in Column B. Write the correct letter on the line.

COLUMN A	COLUMN B
1. Cotton _____	a. raise cotton?
2. Why do farmers _____	b. grow best?
3. People _____	c. need a lot of sun.
4. Where does cotton _____	d. is a plant.
5. Cotton plants _____	e. use cotton to make clothes.

Name _____

3. Question Words

A question often starts with a question word. Some question words are *who*, *what*, *where*, *when*, *why*, and *how*.

Complete each question with *who*, *what*, *when*, *why*, *how*, or *where*. Remember to start each sentence with a capital letter.

1. A lot of wheat is grown in South Dakota.

   _____ is a lot of wheat grown?

2. Wheat grows well there because the soil is rich.

   _____ does wheat grow well there?

3. Wheat farmers plow the fields carefully.

   _____ do wheat farmers plow the fields?

4. Then the farmers plant the wheat seeds.

   _____ plants the wheat seeds?

5. The wheat plants start to grow in the fall.

   _____ starts to grow in the fall?

6. Snow protects the young plants from cold temperatures.

   _____ protects the young plants from cold temperatures?

7. During the spring the snow melts.

   _____ does the snow melt?

8. The melted snow waters the wheat plants.

   _____ waters the wheat plants?

9. In the summer the wheat is harvested.

   _____ is the wheat harvested?

10. People everywhere eat foods made from wheat flour.

    _____ eats foods made from wheat flour?

Name _____

4. Commands

A **command** is a sentence that tells what to do. The subject of a command is *you,* but the subject is not stated in most commands. A command ends with a period.

Open your book.
Read how to do the experiment.

Change each sentence into a command.

1. You can find out how a plant grows toward light.

   _____

2. First you should put a little soil into two old saucers.

   _____

3. Next you should plant three beans on each saucer.

   _____

4. Then you must water the beans so that the soil is moist.

   _____

5. Now you need to find a small box with a lid.

   _____

6. You should cut a small hole in one side.

   _____

7. You must place one saucer in the box and put the lid on the box.

   _____

8. You have to leave the other saucer in the open.

   _____

9. You should water the plants as needed.

   _____

10. You should observe the plants every day to see how they grow.

    _____

Name _____

5. Exclamations

> An exclamation is a sentence that expresses strong or sudden emotion. It ends with an exclamation point.
>
> **She deserves a big thank-you!**

Put the correct punctuation mark (an exclamation point, a period, or a question mark) at the end of each sentence.

1. Have you heard of Jane Addams

2. She was born in 1860

3. She wanted to be a doctor, but she wasn't healthy enough

4. In 1888 she moved to Chicago

5. Many people in the city were very poor

6. Living conditions were horrible

7. Addams wanted to help, so she started Hull House

8. What was Hull House

9. It was a place where people could go to get help

10. Hull House had a library and an employment office

11. Adults could go to school there at night

12. Addams started the city's first kindergarten there

13. The results of her work were amazing

14. How was Jane Addams rewarded for her work against war

15. She was the first American woman to receive the Nobel Peace Prize

Jane Addams worked hard to help people in need. Give an example of how you could help someone in need.

6. Kinds of Sentences

> A sentence can be a **statement**, a **question**, a **command**, or an **exclamation**.

A. Put the correct punctuation mark at the end of each sentence.

1. A neighborhood is a place where people live

2. What is your neighborhood like

3. A community can be made up of neighborhoods

4. A big community has houses, stores, restaurants, and schools

5. A city is made up of many communities

6. What can you find in a city

7. Most cities have offices, stores, and theaters

8. Cities can be really busy

9. A city has factories and parks

10. Would you rather live in a city or on a farm

B. Decide whether each sentence is a statement, a question, a command, or an exclamation. Write your answer on the line.

_____ 1. There are many good restaurants in my community.

_____ 2. Have you ever eaten Thai food?

_____ 3. I like it better than any other food!

_____ 4. My favorite Thai restaurant is Bangkok House.

_____ 5. Go there to try it as soon as you can.

_____ 6. Do you like Mexican food?

_____ 7. Tony's Tacos is near here.

_____ 8. Tony makes the greatest tacos in town!

_____ 9. Eat in my community.

_____ 10. Tacos are delicious!

7. Subjects

> A sentence has a subject and a predicate. The **subject** is who or what the sentence is about. The **simple subject** is usually a noun. It names the person, place, or thing that is talked about. The **complete subject** is the simple subject and any words that describe it.
>
> SENTENCE   Many wild animals live in national parks.
> COMPLETE SUBJECT Many wild animals
> SIMPLE SUBJECT   animals

A. Whom or what is each sentence about?
Underline the complete subject of each sentence.

1. Three tall giraffes eat leaves from the trees.

2. A baby gorilla sleeps in its mother's arms.

3. The sleek brown otters slid down the riverbank.

4. A large male lion roared loudly.

5. The chattering monkeys swing from branches.

6. A big black bear scratched its back on a tree trunk.

7. Two zookeepers were giving an elephant a shower.

8. A family of zebras rested in the shade.

9. The huge hippopotamus lay in a pond.

10. The excited children are watching the seals.

B. Write the best simple subject on each line.

   canary   colt   dog   fish   kitten

1. The little gray _____ is licking its whiskers.

2. A frisky _____ galloped across the field.

3. The _____ is singing in its cage.

4. The big brown _____ caught the stick.

5. My _____ swim in their bowl.

8. Predicates

A sentence has a subject and a predicate. The **predicate** tells what the subject is or does. The **simple predicate** is a verb, a word or words that name an action or a state of being. The **complete predicate** is the simple predicate and any words that describe it.

SENTENCE	Washington, D.C.,	is an exciting city.
COMPLETE PREDICATE		is an exciting city
SIMPLE PREDICATE		is
SENTENCE	The president	lives in Washington, D.C.
COMPLETE PREDICATE		lives in Washington, D.C.
SIMPLE PREDICATE		lives

A. Underline the complete predicate in each sentence.

1. A city can be a noisy place.

2. Airplanes roar loudly overhead.

3. Huge buses rumble to bus stops.

4. Traffic police blow their whistles.

5. Some workers wear earplugs to protect their hearing.

B. Draw a circle around the simple predicate in each sentence.

1. A community provides goods and services.

2. Restaurants and stores sell goods.

3. Police departments and fire departments supply services.

4. Everyone in a community shares the goods and the services.

5. Customers buy tickets for the movies.

6. People take taxis to the airport.

7. Doctors and nurses help sick people.

8. Workers in factories make cars and trucks.

9. Children and teachers study in the library.

10. Mail carriers deliver packages.

9. Combining Predicates

If two sentences have the same subject, the sentences can be combined to make one sentence with one subject and two predicates. A sentence that has two predicates has a **compound predicate**.

TWO SENTENCES WITH THE SAME SUBJECT AND DIFFERENT PREDICATES
Michael poured the water. Michael added the ice.

COMBINING SENTENCES, USING AND TO CONNECT THE PREDICATES
Michael poured the water and added the ice.

A. Underline the verbs in the predicates of each sentence.

1. Astronomers look at planets and study the stars.

2. Chemists experiment with solids and mix liquids.

3. Geologists explore the earth and examine rocks.

4. Botanists discover new plants and give them names.

5. Zoologists watch wildlife in nature and write reports.

B. Each pair of sentences has the same subject.
Combine each pair to make one smooth sentence.

1. Machines make work easier. Machines help get more work done.

_____

2. A pulley is attached to the flagpole. A pulley helps to raise the flag.

_____

3. A lever needs a fulcrum. A lever requires force.

_____

4. Wheels turn. Wheels sometimes squeak.

_____

5. Machines are used every day. Machines work in different ways.

_____

Name _____

10. Combining Subjects

If two sentences have the same predicate, the sentences can be combined to make one sentence with two subjects and one predicate. A sentence with two subjects has a **compound subject**.

TWO SENTENCES WITH DIFFERENT SUBJECTS AND THE SAME PREDICATE
<u>Diane</u> searched the Internet. <u>Kevin</u> searched the Internet.

COMBINING SENTENCES, USING *AND* TO CONNECT THE SUBJECTS
<u>Diane</u> <u>and</u> <u>Kevin</u> searched the Internet.

Each pair of sentences has the same predicate.
Combine each pair to make one smooth sentence.

1. Ashley thought about possible topics. Pat thought about possible topics.

_____

2. Karol investigated swimming. Jack investigated swimming.

_____

3. Claire did the research. Royce did the research.

_____

4. Mari wrote the first draft. Eileen wrote the first draft.

_____

5. Neil edited the story. Evan edited the story.

_____

6. José typed the second draft. Elise typed the second draft.

_____

7. Jay enjoyed doing the writing. Alice enjoyed doing the writing.

_____

8. Lee added pictures to the report. Cheryl added pictures to the report.

_____

9. Karly drew graphs for the report. Jojo drew graphs for the report.

_____

10. Ms. Cardy eagerly read the report. The parents eagerly read the report.

_____

Name _____

11. Combining Sentences

Short sentences about similar ideas are sometimes boring to read. Combine short sentences into one longer sentence, using a comma and the word *and, but,* or *or.* When two sentences are combined into one sentence with a connecting word, the sentence is called a **compound sentence.**

The children planted flowers. Their father watered the lawn.

The children planted flowers, <u>and</u> their father watered the lawn.

Use a comma and the word *and, but,* or *or* to combine each pair of short sentences.

1. Andy cut the grass. Abbey collected the clippings.

_____

2. Ann trimmed the bushes. Mary weeded the flower bed.

_____

3. Flowers are planted around the tree. A fence keeps the rabbits away.

_____

4. A bird feeder is in the maple tree. A squirrel eats the birdseed.

_____

5. Carrots grow near the gate. Raspberries grow along the fence.

_____

6. The evergreen grew more than one foot. The oak tree grew six inches.

_____

7. We ate lunch. Our parents took a nap.

_____

8. I hike in the forest. I walk along the beach.

_____

9. A turtle sat on a log. A duck landed on the pond.

_____

10. The sky was bright blue. The afternoon sun was warm.

_____

Sentences

12. Avoiding Run-on Sentences

A **run-on sentence** is one in which two or more sentences are put together without the proper connector. Some run-on sentences are separated by only a comma. Those run-ons can easily be fixed by adding *and, but,* or *or* after the comma.

RUN-ON SENTENCE   **Some deserts are very hot, many kinds of animals live there.**

COMPOUND SENTENCE   **Some deserts are very hot, but many kinds of animals live there.**

Decide whether each sentence is a run-on or a correctly combined sentence. If it is a run-on, rewrite it as a compound sentence.

1. Cactus wrens live in thorny shrubs, they eat mostly insects.

   _____

2. These wrens can run quickly, they usually fly.

   _____

3. Their nests are lined with feathers or fur, they have long entrances.

   _____

4. Gila monsters find shade under rocks, or they dig burrows.

   _____

5. The desert tortoise lives in sandy deserts, it can live 50 to 80 years.

   _____

6. This tortoise has a hard upper shell, and its tail is very short.

   _____

7. The female tortoise digs a shallow pit, she lays her eggs in it.

   _____

8. She covers the eggs with sand, then she abandons them.

   _____

9. A roadrunner has short wings, it rarely flies.

   _____

10. A roadrunner runs from its enemies, or it crouches and hides.

13. Reviewing Sentences

A. Read each example. Write S on the line if the words form a sentence. Put a period at the end of each sentence.

_____ 1. Mrs. Chase's class took a trip to Washington, D.C., in the spring

_____ 2. They went to the Smithsonian Institution Building

_____ 3. The red castle on the mall

_____ 4. A collection of museums

_____ 5. Everyone enjoyed the visit

B. Read each sentence. Write E on the line if the sentence is an exclamation. Write Q on the line if the sentence is a question. Put the correct punctuation mark at the end of each sentence.

_____ 6. Did the students enjoy the National Air and Space Museum

_____ 7. The old airplanes were amazing

_____ 8. The spaceship was awesome

_____ 9. Did they see the lunar vehicles

_____ 10. Are they going on a trip again next year

C. Complete each question with *who, what, when, why, how,* or *where.*

11. They saw Owney the dog at the National Postal Museum.

_____ did they see Owney?

12. Several authors wrote books about Owney.

_____ wrote books about Owney?

13. The National Museum of American History is closed on Mondays.

_____ is the National Museum of American History closed?

14. The Hope diamond is a huge blue diamond.

_____ is the name of that huge blue diamond?

15. The diamond can be seen in the National Museum of Natural History.

_____ can the diamond be seen?

CONTINUED

Sentences

Sentences

D. Read each sentence. Draw a line to separate the subject and the predicate.

16. Chicago is the third-largest city in the United States.

17. Thousands of tourists visit Chicago every week.

18. Famous architects designed many of the buildings in Chicago.

19. The Architecture Foundation offers tours of downtown landmarks.

20. Wrigley Field is a popular place in the summer.

21. Baseball fans love to watch games there.

22. Navy Pier is another favorite spot for tourists.

23. People walk, bike, or skate along the lake.

24. A Ferris wheel, a children's museum, and a theater attract crowds.

25. A big-city vacation can be a lot of fun!

Try It Yourself

Write four sentences about the place where you live. Be sure each sentence expresses a complete thought. Use correct punctuation.

_____

_____

_____

_____

Check Your Own Work

Choose a piece of writing from your portfolio, a work in progress, an assignment from another class, or a letter. Revise it, using the skills you have reviewed. This checklist will help you.

✔ Does each sentence express a complete thought?

✔ Does each sentence start with a capital letter?

✔ Does each sentence end with the correct punctuation mark?

Name _____

14. Nouns

> A **noun** is a word that names a person, a place, or a thing.
>
> | PERSON | PLACE | THING |
> |---|---|---|
> | **Meriwether Lewis** | **Montana** | **trail** |

A. Decide if the noun in the first column is a person, a place, or a thing. Circle the correct answer.

1. boat   person   place   (thing)
2. Thomas Jefferson   (person)   place   thing
3. journals   person   place   (thing)
4. William Clark   (person)   place   thing
5. St. Louis, Missouri   person   (place)   thing

B. Underline the nouns in each sentence.

1. President Thomas Jefferson sent Lewis and Clark to explore the West.

2. Lewis and Clark began the trip in a town named St. Louis, Missouri.

3. They made a journey across the Great Plains and the Rocky Mountains.

4. Lewis and Clark were helped by Sacagawea, a Native American woman.

5. The journals of Lewis and Clark tell the story of the trip.

LEWIS

 Lewis and Clark braved many hardships as they explored the West. Give an example of a time when you overcame hardship in order to complete something.

CLARK

15

15. Proper Nouns and Common Nouns

A **proper noun** names a particular person, place, or thing.
A **common noun** names any one member of a group of persons, places, or things.

PROPER NOUN	COMMON NOUN
Mrs. Buehl	**librarian**

Read each sentence. Circle each proper noun and underline each common noun.

1. My friends like to go to the Denver Public Library.

2. They check out new books every Friday.

3. Kim and Karen mainly read mysteries.

4. Their favorite mystery is *The Boxcar Children*.

5. Jim reads many books by his favorite author, Roald Dahl.

6. Mr. Fuentes, the librarian, helps Jim search the catalog.

7. Almost instantly Jim can see a list of books by Dahl.

8. Joan likes books by Laura Ingalls Wilder and Frances Hodgson Burnett.

9. Burnett wrote the book *The Secret Garden*.

10. The book is about a girl named Mary Lennox.

11. Mary finds a hidden garden at Misselthwaite Manor in the countryside.

12. The public library has many interesting things to do.

13. Malik likes to rent CDs and movies from the library.

14. Jim and Kiera like to perform plays for story time.

15. Many libraries have newspapers from other cities.

16. Singular Nouns and Plural Nouns

> A **singular noun** names one person, place, or thing. A **plural noun** names more than one person, place, or thing.
>
> The plural of most nouns is formed by adding *-s* to the singular.
>
> computer   computers   book   books
>
> The plural of nouns ending in *s, x, z, ch,* and *sh* is formed by adding *-es* to the singular.
>
> dish   dishes   beach   beaches

A. Write the plural form of each noun.

1. bench   _benches_
2. nugget   _nuggets_
3. glass   _glasses_
4. waltz   _waltz_
5. church   _churches_

6. brick   _bricks_
7. icicle   _iciles_
8. peach   _peaches_
9. giraffe   _giraffs_
10. dash   _dashes_

B. Write **S** above each singular noun and **P** above each plural noun. Circle the ending added to each plural noun.

One day a fox was walking in the forest when he spotted several

bunches of grapes hanging from a vine. After jumping several times, he

managed to reach a large bunch. He carried the fruit toward his den.

As the fox passed a lake, he looked down into the water. There

was another fox carrying another bunch of grapes. He couldn't believe

that two foxes could be so lucky. He wanted both bunches! When he

opened his mouth to grab the second bunch, though, his own grapes fell

into the water and disappeared! So the greedy animal had no supper

that night.

17. More Plural Nouns

> To make most nouns plural, you add *-s* or *-es* to the singular form.
> Some nouns that end in *y* are different. To form the plural of a noun
> ending in a consonant followed by *y*, change the *y* to *i* and add *-es*.
>
> | | | | |
> |---|---|---|---|
> | baby | babies | puppy | puppies |
> | city | cities | party | parties |
>
> For nouns ending in a vowel and *y*, just add an *-s*.
>
> | | | | |
> |---|---|---|---|
> | boy | boys | key | keys |
> | ray | rays | toy | toys |

A. Underline the nouns in each sentence. Write S above each singular noun and P above each plural noun.

1. My hobbies include collecting stuffed toys.

2. The puppies are sleeping among the daisies.

3. The boys are catching guppies in the pond.

4. The scientist searched the skies for other galaxies.

5. We picked cherries and strawberries at the farm.

B. Write the plural form for each noun.

1. bunny — bunnies
2. joy — joys
3. library — libraries
4. valley — vallies
5. firefly — fireflies
6. country — country
7. factory — factories
8. story — stories
9. bay — bays
10. copy — copies
11. day — days
12. diary — diaries
13. memory — memories
14. chimney — chimneies
15. lady — ladies
16. dairy — dairies
17. play — plays
18. berry — berries
19. guy — guys
20. jay — jays

18. Irregular Plural Nouns

The plurals of some nouns look different from their singular forms.
Irregular plural nouns do not end in -s or -es.

ox	oxen	child	children
tooth	teeth	foot	feet
mouse	mice	woman	women
goose	geese	man	men

Some nouns have the same form in the plural and in the singular.

sheep	sheep	deer	deer
trout	trout	moose	moose

A. If the noun is singular, write S on the line. If the noun is plural, write P. If the noun can be singular or plural, write SP.

_____ 1. children

_____ 2. deer

_____ 3. mouse

_____ 4. teeth

_____ 5. feet

_____ 6. ox

_____ 7. men

_____ 8. sheep

_____ 9. fish

_____ 10. geese

B. Complete each sentence with the plural of the noun in parentheses.

1. Farmers raise _____ for meat and wool. (sheep)

2 They raise _____ for meat and feathers. (goose)

3. Some farmers used to use _____ to pull plows. (ox)

4. Several kinds of _____ are raised on farms. (salmon)

5. Cats chase _____ from farmers' barns. (mouse)

6. Those _____ are veterinarians. (man)

7. They are checking the horse's _____. (foot)

8. They will also check its _____. (tooth)

9. These _____ are studying wildlife. (woman)

10. They want to keep _____ from eating the crops. (deer)

19. Singular Possessive Nouns

A **singular possessive noun** shows that one person or thing possesses, or owns, something. To form the singular possessive, add an apostrophe and the letter s (-'s) to a singular noun.

NOUN	SINGULAR POSSESSIVE NOUN
baker	**baker's oven**
Zach	**Zach's trophy**

A. Circle the possessive noun in each sentence.

1. (Dad's) garden is full of tomatoes, onions, and cilantro.
2. My (mom's) recipe for salsa calls for all of those ingredients.
3. First she cuts up about three of (Dad's) garden tomatoes.
4. She makes sure the (knife's) blade is sharp, so that it cuts easily.
5. Second she dices an onion and puts it into (Aunt Cele's) favorite bowl.
6. My (father's) cilantro will taste great in the salsa.
7. Next I mix the ingredients with a little salt and pepper before adding (Mr. Black's) award-winning jalapeño peppers.
8. My (sister's) friend is able to eat an entire jalapeño pepper.
9. (Teresa's) tongue hurts when the pepper seeds touch it.
10. I plan to make this salsa for our (town's) Mexican fiesta next week.

B. Rewrite each group of words, making the italicized noun into a possessive noun.

Example

the nose of the *clown* _____ the clown's nose _____

100 %

1. the recipe of the *chef* ___the chef's recipe___
2. the plate of the *customer* ___the customer's plate___
3. the meal of the *president* ___the president's meal___
4. the laughter from the *guest* ___the guest's laughter___
5. the cookie of the *child* ___the child's cookie___

Nouns

20. Plural Possessive Nouns

A **plural possessive noun** shows that more than one person or thing owns something. To form the plural possessive of most nouns, change the singular noun into a plural noun and add an apostrophe (') after the -s of the plural form.

SINGULAR	PLURAL	PLURAL POSSESSIVE
boy	boys	boys'
bench	benches	benches'

A. Write the plural form and the plural possessive form of each noun.

100%

	PLURAL	PLURAL POSSESSIVE
1. hen	hens	hens'
2. mother	mothers	mothers'
3. factory	factories	factories'
4. hiker	hikers	hikers'
5. church	churches	churches'
6. student	students	students'
7. teacher	teachers	teachers'
8. puppy	puppies	puppies'
9. musician	musicians	musicians'
10. watch	watches	watches'

B. Complete each sentence with the plural possessive form of the noun in parentheses.

100%

1. My _brothers'_ hobby is raising rabbits. (brother)
2. The _rabbits'_ homes are in the backyard. (rabbit)
3. Their _hutches'_ floors are warm and dry. (hutch)
4. The _bunnies'_ ears wiggle. (bunny)
5. The _boys'_ pets are happy. (boy)

Nouns

21. Irregular Plural Possessive Nouns

The plural forms of irregular nouns do not end in -s. To form the plural possessive of irregular nouns, change the singular noun into a plural noun and add an apostrophe and the letter s (-'s) to the plural form.

SINGULAR	PLURAL	PLURAL POSSESSIVE
man	men	men's
goose	geese	geese's
woman	women	women's

A. Write the plural form and the plural possessive form of each noun.

	PLURAL	PLURAL POSSESSIVE
1. mouse	*maicees*	*mice's*
2. policewoman	*policewomens*	*policewomen's*
3. child	*children*	*childrens'*
4. deer	*deer*	*deers'*
5. salmon	*salmen*	*salmens'*
6. tooth	*teeth*	*teeths'*
7. fireman	*firemen*	*firemens'*
8. sheep	*sheeps*	*sheeps'*
9. foot	*feets*	*feets'*
10. ox	*oxens*	*oxens'*

B. Rewrite each group of words. Insert apostrophes to show plural possession. Be careful. Some nouns are regular plurals, and some nouns are irregular plurals.

Example
salmons fins   salmon's fins

1. policemens hats   *policemen's hats*
2. blue jays nests   *blue jay's nests*
3. libraries computers _____
4. sheeps wool _____
5. childrens game _____

Name _____

22. Singular Possessive Nouns and Plural Possessive Nouns

A. Each of these sentences contains at least one possessive noun. Read each sentence. Underline each singular possessive noun and circle each plural possessive noun.

1. Everyone likes to work in Ms. Price's school store.

2. Ali's job is to stock the store with paper, pencils, erasers, and other supplies.

3. Jane takes the students' orders and fills them.

4. Robert takes each child's money and gives change if necessary.

5. The workers have the principal's and the teachers' trust that they will operate the store properly.

B. Complete each sentence with the singular possessive of the noun given.

dog   1. The _____ bark was worse than its bite.

Anna   2. _____ paints spilled onto the floor.

snake   3. I saw the _____ forked tongue.

Josh   4. _____ firefighter hat had a light on it.

man   5. The _____ glasses were too big for him.

C. Complete each sentence with the plural possessive of the noun given.

clown   1. The _____ costumes were bright yellow and green.

woman   2. Did you find the _____ department?

lawyer   3. All of the _____ offices are on the fifth floor.

shark   4. I don't want to see any _____ teeth.

veterinarian   5. _____ patients might have fur, hair, scales, or feathers.

23

Nouns

23. Collective Nouns

A noun that names a group of things or people is called a **collective noun.**

audience	club	flock	pack
army	crew	group	pair
band	crowd	herd	swarm
class	family	litter	team

A collective noun usually goes with an action word that ends in *-s* in the present tense.

The crowd roars.
Our class takes field trips.

A. Underline the collective noun or nouns in each sentence.

1. The scout troop is camping in the woods.

2. A flock of sheep is in the field.

3. The crew hauled up the sails.

4. My dog had a litter of puppies.

5. My family went to hear the band play.

6. Our club visited a farm that had a colony of bees.

7. The audience stood and cheered for the team.

8. I couldn't see over the crowd.

9. A group of scientists watched the pack of wolves.

10. That farmer owns a herd of cattle.

B. Complete each sentence with a collective noun from the list above.

1. My soccer ____team____ won the game! 100

2. Julio plays guitar in a ____band____.

3. A ____flock____ of geese flew over the pond.

4. The art ____club____ made posters for the concert.

5. This kitten is the cutest one in the ____litter____.

24. Nouns as Subjects

A noun may be used as the subject of a sentence. The **subject** tells what the sentence is about. It tells who or what does something.

Janet rubbed the dog's ears.
The <u>dog</u> wagged its tail.

A. Look at each sentence. Underline each noun that is a subject.

1. Kim pointed to the old house.

2. A light bobbed past the window.

3. Shadows flickered on the curtains.

4. Tall trees shaded the porch.

5. The wind rustled the leaves.

6. The children huddled on the sidewalk.

7. Yan climbed the steps and rang the bell.

8. The door opened slowly.

9. A woman called, "Who's there?"

10. Kenny yelled, "Trick or treat!"

B. Complete each sentence with a noun. You may add other words such as *a* or *the.*

1. _____ ran across the field.

2. _____ floated in the sky.

3. _____ took some sandwiches out of the basket.

4. _____ tasted delicious.

5. _____ watched everything that happened.

25. Words Used as Nouns and Verbs

> Many words can be used both as nouns and as verbs. In the first sentence, *copy* is used as a noun. In the second sentence, it is used as a verb.
>
> **Please print a <u>copy</u> of the letter.**
> **<u>Copy</u> these sentences on your paper.**

If the underlined word is a noun, write **N** on the line. If it is a verb, write **V** on the line.

_N_ 1. I think I passed the <u>test</u>.

_V_ 2. Please <u>test</u> the batteries in the smoke alarm.

_____ 3. Kangaroos <u>leap</u> high.

_____ 4. The dog made a <u>leap</u> for the stick.

_____ 5. The scout troop often puts on <u>plays</u>.

_____ 6. My kitten <u>plays</u> with her catnip mouse.

_____ 7. Would you <u>bait</u> my hook?

_____ 8. We're using worms for <u>bait</u>.

_____ 9. The audience <u>claps</u> for the performers.

_____ 10. There were two loud <u>claps</u> of thunder.

_____ 11. Let's <u>vote</u> for the smartest person.

_____ 12. Nico cast his <u>vote</u> for Keith.

_____ 13. Hand me the hammer and the <u>nails</u>.

_____ 14. The <u>nails</u> on his right hand are dirty.

_____ 15. The carpenter <u>nails</u> the boards together.

26. Reviewing Nouns

A. Decide whether each noun is common or proper and if the noun names a person, a place, or a thing.
Write *common* or *proper* on the first line.
Write *person, place,* or *thing* on the second line.

1. Daniel Boone _____ _____

2. spoons _____ _____

3. pencil _____ _____

4. library _____ _____

5. Miguel _____ _____

6. Jody's Diner _____ _____

7. carpenter _____ _____

8. Krispy Krunchy Fish _____ _____

9. flowers _____ _____

10. park _____ _____

B. Circle the collective noun in each sentence.

11. The band will march in the parade.

12. My family helped look for the lost dog.

13. I hope our baseball team wins today.

14. A swarm of bees chased me across the park.

15. The audience cheered for the actors.

LOST
DOG

CONTINUED

27

Name _____

C. Write the plural form of each singular noun.

16. cobweb _____   21. toy _____

17. house _____   22. puppy _____

18. mouse _____   23. sheep _____

19. goose _____   24. lunch _____

20. fox _____   25. foot _____

D. Rewrite each group of words, using a possessive noun.

26. the books of Tom   _____

27. the fur of the bunnies   _____

28. the shoes of the boys   _____

29. the web of the spider   _____

30. the hats of the women   _____

Try It Yourself
Write a sentence for each kind of noun listed. Check for capital letters and the correct use of apostrophes.

Common Noun _____

Proper Noun _____

Collective Noun _____

Singular Possessive Noun _____

Plural Possessive Noun _____

Check Your Own Work
Choose a piece of writing from your portfolio, a work in progress, an assignment from another class, or a letter. Revise it, using the skills you have reviewed. This checklist will help you.

✔ Have you capitalized all proper nouns?

✔ Have you used apostrophes to show ownership?

✔ In each plural possessive, is the apostrophe in the right place?

Name _____

27. Singular Pronouns

> A **personal pronoun** is a word that takes the place of a noun. A singular personal pronoun refers to one person, place, or thing.
> The singular personal pronouns are *I, me, mine, you, yours, he, him, his, she, her, hers, it,* and *its.*
>
> **The cat jumped down from the roof.**
> **It jumped down from the roof.**
>
> **The flowers were for Carol.**
> **The flowers were for her.**

Write on the line the pronoun that takes the place of the word or words in *italics.*

She 1. *Laura Ingalls* was born in the big woods of Wisconsin.

her 2. The Little House series of books was written by *Laura.*

She 3. *Laura* wrote about life in a pioneer family in the late 1800s.

him 4. Laura and her sisters called *their father* Pa.

he 5. *Pa* took the family from Wisconsin to Kansas in a covered wagon.

it 6. Grasshoppers destroyed *the wheat crop* one year.

her 7. A hard winter of blizzards kept *Laura* inside from October to May.

She 8. *Laura* worked as a teacher 12 miles from home.

him 9. Laura married *Almanzo Wilder.*

it 10. *Life* was difficult on the prairie.

Laura had **courage** throughout her hard life on the prairie. Give an example of a situation in which you showed **courage**.

28. Plural Pronouns

A plural personal pronoun refers to more than one person, place, or thing.

The plural personal pronouns are *we, us, ours, they, them, theirs, you,* and *yours. You* and *yours* can be plural or singular.

Mom and Dad went to the bakery.
They went to the bakery.

A. Circle the plural pronoun or plural pronouns in each sentence.

1. (They) ate bagels for breakfast.
2. (We) put strawberry jelly on the bagels.
3. The toasted sesame bagel was for (them).
4. Can (you two) share the cream cheese with (each other)?
5. Are the cinnamon bagels for (us)?
6. (We) love to put butter and honey on bagels.
7. Mom gave (us) the knife for the butter.
8. Todd and Scott, do (you) work at the bakery?
9. (They) came late to breakfast.
10. (We) saved some bagels for them.

B. Write on the line a pronoun to take the place of the word(s) in *italics.*

__they__ 1. *Carl and I* didn't understand the problem.

__us__ 2. Will someone explain the answer to *Sheila and me?*

__them__ 3. Mrs. Bosnak gave *you and Kiya* some help with the problem.

__them__ 4. I'm glad the teacher didn't ask *Joel and Harry* to solve the problem.

__they__ 5. *Most students* did the problem yesterday.

Pronouns

29. Subject Pronouns

Some personal pronouns may be used as the subjects of sentences. Those pronouns are called **subject pronouns**. The subject pronouns are *I, we, you, he, she, it,* and *they.*

> <u>We</u> liked the video.
> <u>She</u> bought a skirt.

A. Circle the correct subject pronoun in each sentence.

1. (Us We) expect company today.
2. (He Him) fixed the clock so it would work again.
3. Dad and (her she) will take the food to the picnic table.
4. (Them They) are going on a field trip.
5. (We Us) went horseback riding on the farm.
6. Carol and (I me) played checkers with Bruce.
7. (They Them) watched the parade go by.
8. (He Him) slid down the hill on a sled.
9. Shawn and (I me) raced to the beach.
10. (Her She) missed the train.

B. Write on the first line a subject pronoun to take the place of the word or words in *italics.* On the second line write **S** if the pronoun is singular or **P** if it is plural.

	PRONOUN	S OR P
1. Dad said, "*Mom and Sue* should shop at the Big T."	_____	_____
2. *Sue* showed Mom a robot at the store.	_____	_____
3. *The robot* was on sale.	_____	_____
4. "*Dad* would like the robot," Sue said.	_____	_____
5. *Sue's mother and Sue* decided to buy it for him.	_____	_____

30. Object Pronouns

Some personal pronouns may be used after the verb in a sentence. They are called **object pronouns.** The object pronouns are *me, us, you, him, her, it,* and *them.*

> **Dad promised <u>me</u> an ice cream cone.**
> **Greg sent <u>her</u> a thank-you note.**

A. Circle the correct pronoun in parentheses. On the line write an **S** if the pronoun is singular or **P** if it is plural.

_____ 1. Mother gave pasta to (we us).

_____ 2. We ate (they it) with delight.

_____ 3. It was the same kind of pasta
   that Mom gave (we you), Anthony.

_____ 4. Mother feeds (he him) well.

_____ 5. Anthony loves (she her) for it.

_____ 6. Mother likes fruit and thinks dinner should end with (him it).

_____ 7. Mother makes baked apples and gives them to (we us).

_____ 8. Vittorio and I taste (they them) with delight.

_____ 9. By the end of dinner, there are many dishes in front of (I me).

_____ 10. I offered to wash (they them).

B. On the line write a pronoun that takes the place of the word or words in *italics.* Use pronouns that usually come after a verb.

_____ 1. I asked *Tom* to hold the sunscreen.

_____ 2. Lisa told *Tom and Jake* to put some of it on.

_____ 3. Tom and Jake saved enough sunscreen for *Lisa and me.*

_____ 4. The sun burned *Jake* anyway.

_____ 5. Jake told *Lisa* that the burn really hurt.

Pronouns

31. Possessive Pronouns

Possessive pronouns show who or what owns something. The possessive pronouns are *mine, ours, yours, his, hers, its,* and *theirs.*

> The hat is <u>mine</u>.
> Is that house <u>theirs</u>?

A. Match the object owned in Column A with the correct possessive pronoun in Column B. Write the letter on the line. Some possessive pronouns are used more than once.

COLUMN A	COLUMN B
_c_ 1. my house	a. yours
_f_ 2. her scooter	b. ours
_a_ 3. your kitten	c. mine
_e_ 4. Tom's bike	d. theirs
_d_ 5. Megan and Josh's boat	e. his
___ 6. my family's cabin	f. hers
___ 7. Miss Tower's lawn	
___ 8. Mr. Allen's motorcycle	
___ 9. your vacation	
___ 10. the children's toys	

B. Complete each sentence with a possessive pronoun: *mine, ours, yours, his, hers,* or *theirs.* Do not use the same pronoun in every sentence.

1. Where are _____?

2. I took _____ by mistake.

3. _____ are worn out.

4. Take _____ to the library.

5. The polka dots on _____ are green and yellow.

32. Possessive Adjectives

An adjective is a word that describes a noun. *My, our, your, his, her, its,* and *their* are adjectives that go before nouns to show ownership. They are called **possessive adjectives**.

I lost <u>my</u> sunscreen.
Did you bring <u>your</u> beach ball?

A. Circle the possessive adjective in each sentence.

1. Our family took a trip to the lake.

2. I wore my new swimsuit.

3. Laura brought her sunglasses.

4. Dad carried his fishing pole.

5. Where's your hat, Mike?

6. Mike and Laura dipped their toes in the lake.

7. Its water was cool and inviting.

8. Mom and Dad, your towels are over here.

9. I caught my first fish.

10. We all enjoyed our afternoon.

B. Complete each sentence with a possessive adjective.

1. Laura bought _____ sunglasses at the mall.

2. Mike left _____ hat in the car.

3. _____ new swimsuit is blue.

4. Mom and Dad ate _____ sandwiches.

5. We picked up _____ trash before we left.

33. Agreement of Pronouns and Verbs

A subject and its verb must agree. When *he, she,* or *it* is the subject, add an *-s* to the present tense form of the verb.

I like cats.	She likes dogs.
We raise horses.	He raises cattle.
They eat oats.	It eats hay.

A. Circle the verb that agrees with the subject pronoun.

1. She (own owns) a horse.

2. They (train trains) the horse every day.

3. He (give gives) it oats and water.

4. We (watch watches) her ride.

5. It (trot trots) around the ring.

6. You (need needs) a firm grip to be a good rider.

7. I (ride rides) with her often.

8. She (win wins) prizes in shows.

9. They (award awards) them to the best riders.

10. He (feel feels) proud of her.

B. Complete each sentence with a subject pronoun. Be sure the subject pronoun and the verb agree.

1. _____ wash the car every Saturday.

2. _____ wipes the windows.

3. _____ clean the tires.

4. _____ polishes the hood.

5. _____ shines in the sun.

Pronouns

34. *I* and *Me*

> *I* is used as the subject of a sentence.
> *I* is a subject pronoun.
> *Me* is usually used after the verb.
> *Me* is an object pronoun.
>
> **I love going to the aquarium.**
> **Dad saw me wave.**

Pronouns

A. Circle the correct pronoun in parentheses.

1. Mom and (I me) went to the supermarket.

2. Rita saw my mom and (I me) shopping.

3. Mom asked (I me) what I wanted for dinner.

4. (I Me) wanted tacos and salad.

5. Mom told (I me) to find the taco shells in aisle four.

6. (I Me) asked whether we could have soda pop with dinner.

7. She told (I me) that fruit juice would be better.

8. She asked (I me) to get some fresh raspberries for dessert.

9. (I Me) really liked the tacos my mom made.

10. (I Me) said, "My mom and (I me) are a good team!"

B. Complete each sentence with *I* or *me*.

1. Terry called _____ yesterday after school.

2. He asked _____ to go for a bike ride.

3. _____ was glad to join him.

4. Terry asked _____ to meet him at the park.

5. Terry and _____ had a good time.

35. Compound Subjects

> Pronouns can be used in compound subjects. The subject pronouns are *I, you, he, she, it, we,* and *they.*
>
> **Mom, Dad, and <u>I</u> cleaned out the garage.**
> **<u>He</u> and <u>she</u> moved their cars.**

A. **Circle the correct pronoun or pronouns for each sentence.**

1. Dad and (I me) made shelves for the cleaning supplies.

2. (He him) and Mom recycled the old newspapers.

3. Dylan and (her she) sorted all the sporting equipment.

4. (Them They) and Dad hung the tools on the wall.

5. Grace and (he him) put all the toys into bins.

6. (We Us) and Mom washed the windows.

7. (Her She) and Dad made a space for the gardening supplies.

8. (He Him) and (I me) swept the floor carefully.

9. (Us We) and the neighbors put our trash at the curb.

10. (They them) and (us we) were pleased.

B. **Complete each sentence with a subject pronoun or pronouns.**

1. Mom and _____ made potato salad.

2. _____ and Brian set up the grill.

3. _____ and _____ washed the patio furniture.

4. _____ and Dad started the fire.

5. _____ and the neighbors grilled hamburgers.

36. Compound Objects

> Pronouns can be used as compound objects. The object pronouns are *me, you, him, her, it, us,* and *them.*
>
> **Rachel helped Mitch and <u>me</u> with the homework.**
> **I showed <u>him</u> and <u>her</u> how to use fractions.**

A. Circle the correct pronoun or pronouns for each sentence.

1. Mrs. Harris hired Brad and (I me) to babysit her son and daughter.

2. We dressed (she her) and (he him) in warm clothes.

3. I pulled Brad and (them they) on a sled.

4. Brad showed (they them) and (I me) how to make snow angels.

5. We helped (him he) and (her she) make a snow fort.

6. Connie joined (them they) and (we us) in a snowball fight.

7. They hit (her she) and (us we) with snowballs.

8. We took (he him) and (her she) back home.

9. Mrs. Harris made (they them) and (us we) hot soup for lunch.

10. She paid Brad and (me I) for helping with the children.

B. Complete each sentence with an object pronoun or pronouns.

1. Dad and Mom asked my friends and _____ to rake the yard.

2. We've helped _____ and _____ before.

3. Dad showed Mike and _____ the new rake.

4. He helped _____ and _____ put the leaves in a bag.

5. Mom thanked _____ and _____ for helping.

37. Reviewing Pronouns

A. Circle the pronoun or pronouns in each sentence.

1. We saw a small lizard.

2. It jumped to a rock near me.

3. She drew pictures of it.

4. We always carry them.

5. I drew some pictures of it too.

B. Name the subject pronoun that would take the place of the word or words in *italics*. Write your answer on the line.

_____ 6. *Melissa* plays the cello.

_____ 7. *Joe and Beth* practice playing guitar together.

_____ 8. *Billy* is learning a song to play on the piano.

_____ 9. *Mara and I* prefer playing the trumpet to playing the tuba.

_____ 10. *The tuba* is large and heavy.

C. Name a pronoun that would take the place of the word or words in *italics* that follow the verb. Write your answer on the line.

_____ 11. Put *the camera* on the tripod.

_____ 12. Mom asked *Jeff and Betsy* to smile.

_____ 13. Jeff told *Betsy* something funny.

_____ 14. The camera wasn't pointing toward *Dad and me*.

_____ 15. I took a picture of *Dad* at the top of the canyon.

D. Underline the possessive pronoun or pronouns in each sentence.

16. That book of folktales is his.

17. Carolyn's folktale came from the same country as mine.

18. Hers came from France.

19. Is yours an African folktale?

20. Theirs is more interesting than ours.

E. Complete each sentence with *I* or *me*.

21. Keri and _____ read "The Shepherd and the Princess."

22. _____ enjoy reading folktales.

23. Keri told Colleen and _____ that "The Three Magi" was her favorite story.

24. Colleen asked _____ to read it to her.

25. _____ enjoyed reading it aloud.

Try It Yourself
Write three sentences about a book that you have liked or disliked. Use pronouns, including possessive pronouns. Be sure to use *I* and *me* correctly.

_____

_____

_____

Check Your Own Work
Choose a piece of writing from your portfolio, a work in progress, an assignment for another class, or a letter. Revise it, using the skills you have reviewed. This checklist will help you.

✔ Have you used pronouns in place of nouns?

✔ Have you used possessive pronouns to show who owns something?

✔ Have you used *I* and *me* correctly?

Name _____

38. Verbs

> A predicate always has a verb. A **verb** tells what someone or something does or what someone or something is.
>
> **The doctor talks with patients.**
> **The shirt is blue and white.**

100 %

Circle the verbs in the following sentences.

1. Agnes Gonxha Bojaxhiu joined a religious order in 1928.

2. She took the name of Teresa.

3. Then she moved to India.

4. Teresa worked as a history and geography teacher.

5. In a hospital there she helped sick and hungry mothers.

6. Later she lived among the poorest of the poor people.

7. She started the Missionaries of Charity in India.

8. The Missionaries of Charity help people who are in need.

9. Mother Teresa died in September 1997.

10. Even now Mother Teresa's Missionaries of Charity continue her work around the world.

 Mother Teresa dedicated her life to helping the poorest people. Give an example of what you could do to help someone.

39. Action Verbs

Action verbs express action.

   Fish <u>swim</u>.   Spiders <u>spin</u>.   Artists <u>paint</u>.

Read this poem. Write action verbs from the poem to complete the sentences below.

How Creatures Move
A lion walks on padded paws;
Squirrels leap from limb to limb.
A crab runs with two pinchy claws,
And seals can dive and swim.
Some monkeys swing with twisty tails
High up in the trees,
And birds can spread their wings and sail
Or hop on lawns with ease.
Boy and girls hop too, you know.
Kids all play games for fun.
Just like merry animals,
They leap and prance and run.

1. The lion <u>walks</u>.

2. Squirrels <u>leap</u>.

3. A crab <u>runs</u>.

4. Seals can <u>dive</u> and <u>swim</u>.

5. Monkeys <u>swing</u>.

6. Birds can <u>spread</u> their wings and <u>sail</u> among the treetops.

7. Birds may also <u>hop</u> on the ground.

8. Boys and girls <u>hop</u> too.

9. Kids <u>play</u> games for fun.

10. They <u>leap</u> and <u>prance</u> and <u>run</u>.

Verbs

40. More Action Verbs

> Action verbs tell what happens.
>
> **My aunt <u>hikes</u> in the mountains for exercise.**
> **Roxanna <u>reads</u> a book every week.**

A. Circle the action verbs in this story about a boy in Iowa.

Andy (lives) on a farm in Iowa. His family (raises) dairy cows and (grows) corn. Andy's father (milks) the cows every morning and every evening. The family (sells) the milk to a dairy. *100%*

B. Complete each sentence with an action verb from the list. Use each verb once. *100%*

~~live~~   ~~looks~~   ~~finds~~   ~~sail~~   ~~travels~~

1. Tara __looks__ at a map of the world.

2. She __finds__ Egypt on the map.

3. Tara __travels__ to Egypt to see her grandparents.

4. They __live__ near the Nile River.

5. Boats __sail__ up and down this great river.

~~rides~~   ~~study~~   ~~sleep~~   ~~visit~~   ~~photographs~~   *100%*

6. Tara and her grandparents __visit__ the great pyramids.

7. Tourists carefully __study__ the pictures on the pyramid walls.

8. Grandfather __photographs__ the Sphinx.

9. Grandmother __rides__ in the tour bus.

10. Tara and her grandparents __sleep__ in a hotel.

Verbs

41. Being Verbs

A **being verb** shows what someone or something is. Being verbs do not express action. Some being verbs are *am, is, are, was, were, be, has been, had been, have been, and will be.*

Paulo and Ricardo <u>are</u> good at Internet searches.
Information about earthquakes <u>is</u> on the Internet.

A. Circle the verb in each sentence. On the line write A if the verb is an action verb or B if it is a being verb.

_B_ 1. Earthquakes (are) movements in plates of land.

_A_ 2. We (call) a huge piece of land a *plate.*

_B_ 3. Plates (are) like pieces of a large puzzle.

_B_ 4. A fault line (is) a crack in the ground between two plates.

_A_ 5. Pressure at fault lines (causes) earthquakes.

B. Put a check in front of each sentence that uses a being verb. Circle all being verbs.

_✓_ 1. Earthquakes (are) possible in many parts of the world.

_____ 2. Landslides during earthquakes (damage) buildings, roads, and homes.

_____ 3. Fires start from (broken) fuel lines and electric cables.

_✓_ 4. California (is) the site of many earthquakes.

_____ 5. The Richter scale (measures) the size and strength of earthquakes.

_✓_ 6. There (is) no way to stop an earthquake.

_____ 7. Scientists cannot predict an earthquake very well.

_✓_ 8. Earthquakes (are) (dangerous) natural events.

_✓_ 9. Tornadoes and hurricanes (are) also natural events.

_✓_ 10. Earthquakes (will be) a part of nature forever.

Verbs

42. Helping Verbs

A verb can have two parts—a helping verb and a main verb. A **helping verb** is a verb added before the main verb to make the meaning clear. Some helping verbs are *am, is, are, was, were, be, been, do, does, has, have, had, will, can,* and *might.*

Our class <u>has worked</u> on many art projects.

The helping verb is *has.* The main verb is *worked.*

A. Circle the helping verb or verbs in each sentence.

1. Bernadette was working on a magnet experiment.

2. She is checking whether her magnet will attract paper clips through cardboard.

3. Magnetic fields were found surrounding planets.

4. My compass might have a magnet inside.

5. Electricity will make a piece of iron wrapped in wire into a magnet.

B. Underline the main verb in each sentence.

1. Arturo has investigated energy.

2. He will learn that light is energy from the sun.

3. Batteries can store energy.

4. Some machines will convert stored energy to motion and heat.

5. Water and sound waves can carry energy from one place to another.

C. Circle the helping verb that best completes each sentence.

1. Chen (will been) use a magnifying glass.

2. He (might am) look at a rock with it.

3. Scientists (can have) discovered that some rocks are harder than others.

4. They (is are) making a hypothesis.

5. Lee (will were) test limestone to see whether it cracks.

Verbs

43. Principal Parts of Verbs

A verb has four **principal parts**.

PRESENT	PRESENT PARTICIPLE	PAST	PAST PARTICIPLE
walk	**walking**	**walked**	**walked**

PRESENT PARTICIPLE: a verb that ends in *-ing* and is used with *am, is, are, was,* or *were*

> Harold is <u>unfolding</u> the world map.

PAST: a verb that usually ends in *-d* or *-ed.* It is not used with a helping verb.

> Liam <u>learned</u> the difference between maps and globes.

PAST PARTICIPLE: a verb that usually ends in *-d* or *-ed.* It is used with *has, have,* or *had.*

> He has <u>used</u> the scale to measure distances.

For each verb in *italics,* write present, past, or past participle on the line.

_____ 1. The twins have *measured* the distance on the map from New York City to Los Angeles.

_____ 2. Once students *understand* the map scale, the distance is easy to figure out.

_____ 3. Our visitors *used* a globe to point out the Amazon River in South America.

_____ 4. Karim has *remembered* that the Himalaya Mountains are in northern India.

_____ 5. He *locates* them by using the map legend.

_____ 6. The compass has *helped* the class decide which way is north.

_____ 7. Northern countries *include* Russia, Finland, and Canada.

_____ 8. The grid on the map *helped* us compare the sizes of countries.

_____ 9. Each group has *traced* the map of a different state.

_____ 10. The United States of America *is* in the Northern Hemisphere.

Verbs

44. Regular and Irregular Verbs

> The past and the past participle of **regular verbs** usually end in *-d* or *-ed*.
> The past and the past participle of irregular verbs are not formed by adding *-d* or *-ed* to the present.
> The past participle is always used with *have, has,* or *had.*
>
> *Clean* is a regular verb.
>   PRESENT: **clean**   PAST: **cleaned**   PAST PARTICIPLE: **(has) cleaned**
>
> *Go* is an irregular verb.
>   PRESENT: **go**   PAST: **went**   PAST PARTICIPLE: **(has) gone**

Verbs

A. Complete the chart of regular verbs.

PRESENT	PAST		PAST PARTICIPLE
1. wash	washed	(has)	washed
2. talk	talked	(has)	talked
3. review	reviewed	(has)	reviewed
4. yell	yelled	(has)	yelled
5. trick	tricked	(has)	tricked

B. Complete the chart of irregular verbs.

PRESENT	PAST		PAST PARTICIPLE
1. give	gave	(have)	given
2. see	saw	(have)	seen
3. sit	sat	(have)	sat
4. come	came	(have)	come
5. write	wrote	(have)	written

C. Write whether each verb in *italics* is regular or irregular.

_____ 1. My brother has *fed* our dog every day this week.

_____ 2. I have *brushed* her.

_____ 3. We *take* the dog to the groomer, Mr. Charles, today.

_____ 4. Mr. Charles has *worked* in town for years.

_____ 5. He has *put* a bow on the dog's crate after each visit.

Name _LucyM M._

45. Bring

Bring is an irregular verb. These are the principal parts of bring.

PRESENT	PRESENT PARTICIPLE	PAST	PAST PARTICIPLE
bring	bringing	brought	brought

The present participle is used with a helping verb such as *am, is, are, was,* or *were.*

The past participle is used with a helping verb such as *has, have,* or *had.*

Verbs

A. Complete each sentence with the correct form of *bring*.

1. ___Bring___ up local problems with your city government.

2. The students ___brought___ the river pollution problem to the mayor.

3. Others have ___brought___ this same issue to the city council.

4. The mayor has ___brought___ in experts to talk about the need for clean rivers.

5. Some students are ___bringing___ trash bags, rakes, and gloves to clean up the riverbank.

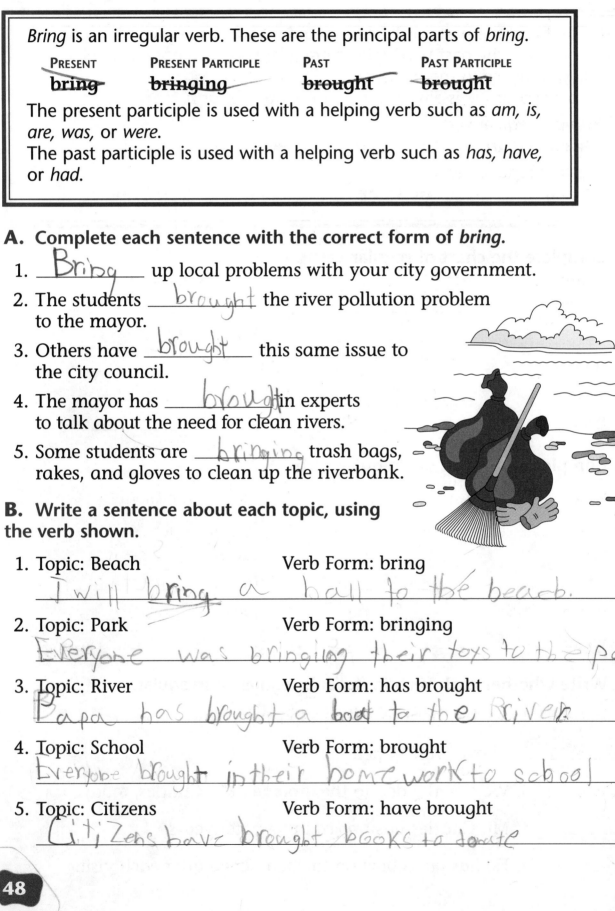

B. Write a sentence about each topic, using the verb shown.

1. Topic: Beach   Verb Form: bring

   I will bring a ball to the beach.

2. Topic: Park   Verb Form: bringing

   Everyone was bringing their toys to the park.

3. Topic: River   Verb Form: has brought

   Papa has brought a boat to the River

4. Topic: School   Verb Form: brought

   Everyone brought in their homework to school

5. Topic: Citizens   Verb Form: have brought

   Citizens have brought books to donate

Name _____

46. *Buy*

> *Buy* is an irregular verb. These are the principal parts of *buy*.
>
> | PRESENT | PRESENT PARTICIPLE | PAST | PAST PARTICIPLE |
> |---------|--------------------|------|-----------------|
> | **buy** | **buying** | **bought** | **bought** |
>
> The present participle is used with a helping verb such as *am, is, are, was,* or *were.*
> The past participle is used with a helping verb such as *has, have,* or *had.*

A. Complete each sentence with the correct form of *buy*.

1. Will you __buy__ a book to donate to the library?

2. Last year my aunt __bought__ a book for the library in honor of my birthday.

3. The class has __bought__ many books for our library in the past.

4. I usually __buy__ a book I want to read.

5. Please __buy__ this book about China.

6. Last year Maureen __bought__ a book about Italy.

7. I am __buying__ that book for myself to keep.

8. If you __buy__ a book for the library, many people can read it.

9. I did not __buy__ a book for myself.

10. I __bought__ a book in order to help the library.

B. For each verb in *italics*, write present, present participle, past, or past participle on the line.

__Past participle__ 1. Some teachers have *bought* special materials for the classroom.

__Past__ 2. Mr. Markin *bought* the best microscope I have ever seen for our class.

__Past__ 3. My gym teacher already *bought* new basketballs.

__Present__ 4. The art teachers *buy* paints for each student.

__present participle__ 5. Sara is *buying* a centimeter ruler for math class.

47. Come

> *Come* is an irregular verb. These are the principal parts of *come*.
>
> | PRESENT | PRESENT PARTICIPLE | PAST | PAST PARTICIPLE |
> |---------|--------------------|------|-----------------|
> | **come** | **coming** | **came** | **come** |
>
> The present participle is used with a helping verb such as *am, is, are, was,* or *were*.
>
> The past participle is used with a helping verb such as *has, have,* or *had*.

Verbs

A. Complete each sentence with the correct form of *come*.

1. Today we have _come_ to the library to research our state.

2. Our class _came_ to research natural resources yesterday.

3. The librarian is _coming_ to tell about reference books.

4. Business leaders have _came_ to talk about what makes our city and state great.

5. People originally _came_ to our city because of the river and the railroad.

6. Tourists often _come_ to our state to enjoy its natural beauty.

7. Of all the classes, ours has _come_ to the library most often.

8. The governor of our state is _comeing_ to visit our community.

9. She had _come_ to visit once before.

10. The governor and the mayor _came_ to our school to talk about transportation last year.

B. Underline the verb that best completes each sentence.

1. Our county treasurer (come (came)) to talk about taxes.

2. The treasurer has ((come) came) to speak to the third grade.

3. Our class (come (came)) to the gym to hear him speak about government in this century.

4. The principal and the librarian have ((come) came) in the past.

5. Will a county judge ((come) came) to talk about laws?

48. *Sit*

> *Sit* is an irregular verb. These are the principal parts of *sit*.
>
> | PRESENT | PRESENT PARTICIPLE | PAST | PAST PARTICIPLE |
> |---------|--------------------|------|-----------------|
> | sit | sitting | sat | sat |
>
> The present participle is used with a helping verb such as *am, is, are, was,* or *were.*
> The past participle is used with a helping verb such as *has, have,* or *had.*

A. Read the following paragraph. Underline the principal parts of *sit*.

We <u>sat</u> in the front row at the circus yesterday. A woman in a sparkly dress was <u>sitting</u> on an elephant's back. A trapeze artist <u>sat</u> on a swing high above the crowd. An animal trainer told a lion, "<u>Sit</u> down, please." The lion <u>sat</u> quietly on a rug.

B. Complete each sentence with the correct form of *sit*.

1. Michaela _sat_ on a plane when she flew to Washington, D.C.

2. Her parents were _siting_ next to her.

3. Tourists often _sit_ in the Capitol to watch laws being made.

4. They are _siting_ in the balcony seats called the gallery.

5. The vice president _sat_ down after he spoke.

6. After a long day the family _sat_ by the hotel pool.

7. Several rocking chairs are _siting_ around the pool.

8. Michaela's mother told her that President Kennedy had _sat_ in a rocking chair to rest his back.

9. President Roosevelt _sat_ in a wheelchair for part of his life.

10. At the Roosevelt Memorial a statue of the president's dog _sat_ next to the president's statue.

Verbs

Name _____

49. *Eat*

> *Eat* is an irregular verb. These are the principal parts of *eat*.
>
> | PRESENT | PRESENT PARTICIPLE | PAST | PAST PARTICIPLE |
> |---------|--------------------|------|-----------------|
> | **eat** | **eating** | **ate** | **eaten** |
>
> The present participle is used with a helping verb such as *am, is, are, was,* or *were.*
> The past participle is used with a helping verb such as *has, have,* or *had.*

A. Complete each sentence with the correct form of *eat*.

1. Good nutrition means that each day people __*eat*__ healthful meals.

2. Yesterday Hailey __*ate*__ rice cakes for a snack.

3. Jee has __*eaten*__ a hot lunch in the cafeteria every day this year.

4. For good health __*eating*__ an apple instead of candy as a snack.

5. Have you __*ate*__ a nutritious lunch?

6. Most children like to __*eat*__ cake at birthday parties.

7. Everyone should try to __*eat*__ fruits and vegetables each day.

8. You can get sick if you have __*ate*__ too much food that is not nutritious.

9. Marty was __*eating*__ a bunch of grapes.

10. Ms. Flores has __*ate*__ green vegetables almost every day of her life.

B. Replace the word in *italics* with *eat, eating, ate,* or *eaten*.

__*ate*__ 1. Humberto and Luz *bring* tortillas.

__*eaten*__ 2. They have *chosen* mild jalapeño peppers.

__*eating*__ 3. Luz is *cooking* only a small portion of corn.

__*eaten*__ 4. Papa has *enjoyed* all of the tostadas.

__*ate*__ 5. Tía Alba *prepared* the spicy bean soup.

Verbs

50. *Go*

Go is an irregular verb. These are the principal parts of *go*.

PRESENT	PRESENT PARTICIPLE	PAST	PAST PARTICIPLE
go	**going**	**went**	**gone**

The present participle is used with a helping verb such as *am, is, are, was,* or *were.*

The past participle is used with a helping verb such as *has, have,* or *had.*

A. Choose the correct form of *go* for each sentence.

1. Please ___go___ to the straw mat, a Kwanzaa symbol of tradition.

2. I am ___going___ to my uncle's house for this African American holiday.

3. Mother has ___went___ to get the seven candles.

4. She ___went___ to the front of the room to tell what each candle means.

5. We ___gont___ to the table each of the seven nights to light one of the candles.

B. Circle the correct form of *go* to complete each sentence.

1. My family and I always (go went gone) to Kwanzaa celebrations.

2. We have (go went gone) to a feast every year that I can remember.

3. We (go went gone) every December 31.

4. Kiandra has (go went gone) with her family.

5. She (go went gone) to celebrate her family's history.

6. Does your family (go going gone) to any special festivals?

7. Each year we have (go going gone) to the ceremony as a family.

8. My best friend is (go going gone) with us this year.

9. I (go went gone) to my first celebration when I was a baby.

10. Are you (go going gone) too?

51. See

See is an irregular verb. These are the principal parts of see.

PRESENT	PRESENT PARTICIPLE	PAST	PAST PARTICIPLE
see	seeing	saw	seen

The present participle is used with a helping verb such as *am, is, are, was,* or *were.*

The past participle is used with a helping verb such as *has, have,* or *had.*

A. Read the following paragraph about California. Underline the principal parts of see.

Residents and tourists have <u>seen</u> the beauty of California. They can <u>see</u> oceans, coastlines, mountains, and valleys. Last year when I visited, I <u>saw</u> the desert. I have <u>seen</u> all of these features on a physical map. My class <u>sees</u> the Sacramento River on the map.

B. Circle the correct form of see in each sentence.

1. Early explorers (see saw (seen)) great wonders in California.

2. Unfortunately, not many of them (see (saw) seen) gold.

3. Many people have (see saw (seen)) the pretty mountains.

4. My grandfather has (see seeing (seen)) new industry begin in California.

5. Mother is (see (seeing) seen) all of her family in Sacramento.

C. Write the correct form of see on each line.

1. You can ___see___ symbols in a medicine wheel.

2. Did you ___see___ the circle that represents the Circle of Life?

3. You have ___seen___ the wooden totem poles.

4. This morning Nadia ___saw___ an eagle.

5. She always feels peaceful after she has ___seen___ an eagle.

52. *Take*

Take is an irregular verb. These are the principal parts of *take*.

PRESENT	PRESENT PARTICIPLE	PAST	PAST PARTICIPLE
take	taking	took	taken

The present participle is used with a helping verb such as *am, is, are, was,* or *were.*

The past participle is used with a helping verb such as *has, have,* or *had.*

A. Complete each sentence with the correct form of *take.*

1. Ruth is _taking_ a tour of memorials in Washington, D.C.

2. Her guide has _took_ time to explain the meaning of each memorial.

3. She _took_ a trip into history at every monument or building.

4. The bus tour of the memorials _took_ two hours.

5. Yesterday some people _took_ a walking tour of the memorials.

6. Justin _took_ a picture of the Lincoln Memorial.

7. Martin Luther King, Jr., has _taken_ a place among American heroes.

8. Martin Luther King, Jr., _took_ civil rights seriously.

9. King spoke out against those who were _taking_ away the rights of African Americans.

10. Americans have _taken_ care to remember his work.

B. Write PR for present, P for past, or PP for past participle over the forms of *take.*

                    P
"Benjamin Franklin took care of people's needs with some of his

                               PR
inventions," my father says as he takes off his glasses. "Franklin made

                                      P
bifocals popular, but some of the work he took part in protects us. You

                        PP
know that he had taken an interest in electricity. Did you know that he

invented lightning rods to protect buildings from fire? He also started the

first fire brigade. Let's take a few minutes to research his other ideas."

53. *Tear*

Tear is an irregular verb. These are the principal parts of *tear*.

PRESENT	PRESENT PARTICIPLE	PAST	PAST PARTICIPLE
tear	**tearing**	**tore**	**torn**

The present participle is used with a helping verb such as *am, is, are, was,* or *were.*

The past participle is used with a helping verb such as *has, have,* or *had.*

A. Underline the form of *tear* in each sentence.

1. The students in Mr. Ito's class are <u>tearing</u> paper for their art projects.

2. Beth carefully <u>tore</u> thin red paper to make a flower.

3. She has also <u>torn</u> green paper to make leaves.

4. She was <u>tearing</u> paper for the stem when the bell rang.

5. She will <u>tear</u> the rest of the paper tomorrow.

B. Circle the correct form of *tear* for each sentence.

1. Those boys are (tear (tearing)) paper to make lion masks.

2. George has ((torn) tore) a sheet of construction paper into a round shape.

3. He ((tore) tear) holes in the paper for eyes.

4. Now he is ((tearing) tore) pieces for the mane.

5. The boys are (tear (tearing)) their paper very carefully.

C. Write the correct form of *tear* on the line.

1. Ana and Sue are __*tearing*__ magazine pages to make collages.

2. They have __*tore*__ different shapes and sizes.

3. You can __*tear*__ the paper into any shapes you like.

4. Earlier, Ana __*tore*__ heavy paper to make a frame.

5. Mr. Ito is __*tearing*__ gold paper to make stars.

Verbs

Name _____

54. *Write*

Write is an irregular verb. These are the principal parts of *write*.

PRESENT	PRESENT PARTICIPLE	PAST	PAST PARTICIPLE
write	**writing**	**wrote**	**written**

The present participle is used with a helping verb such as *am, is, are, was,* or *were.*
The past participle is used with a helping verb such as *has, have,* or *had.*

A. Complete each sentence with the correct form of *write.*

1. Who __wrote__ the Declaration of Independence?

2. Thomas Jefferson had __written__ the first draft 20 years before he became president.

3. Americans __wrote__ the U.S. Constitution to name the basic laws of their new country.

4. Abbey has __written__ a report about the U.S. Constitution.

5. Senators __wrote__ laws for everyone in the country.

6. Members of Congress __write__ laws that are later debated at the U.S. Capitol.

7. Some senators are __writing__ laws about education.

8. Our U.S. representative __wrote__ a law to help the elderly.

9. What laws would you have __wrote__?

10. I __wrote__ letters to the members of Congress from my state.

B. Put a check mark before each statement that is written correctly.

__✓__ 1. Students have written about the Statue of Liberty.

_____ 2. They written how it is a great symbol of freedom.

__✓__ 3. Who wrote about other symbols?

__✓__ 4. Oscar has written about the bald eagle.

_____ 5. Ben and Troy have wrote a poem about the flag.

55. Irregular Verbs

A. Complete the chart of irregular verbs.

PRESENT	PAST	PAST PARTICIPLE
1. bring	_____	(has) _____
2. run	_____	(has) _____
3. eat	_____	(has) _____
4. go	_____	(has) _____
5. sit	_____	(has) _____

B. Complete the chart of irregular verbs.

PAST	PRESENT	PRESENT PARTICIPLE
1. saw	_____	(is) _____
2. bought	_____	(is) _____
3. came	_____	(is) _____
4. took	_____	(is) _____
5. wrote	_____	(is) _____

C. Write a sentence for each verb.

1. give

_____

2. am giving, is giving, or are giving

_____

3. gave

_____

4. has given, have given, or had given

_____

5. was giving or were giving

_____

Verbs

Name _____

56. Simple Present Tense

A verb in the **simple present tense** tells about something that is always true or about an action that happens again and again.

A planet <u>orbits</u> the sun.
Telescopes <u>magnify</u> the stars.

A. Circle the correct verb in each sentence.

1. Earth (move moves) around the Sun.

2. The Sun (provide provides) heat and energy.

3. The Moon (reflect reflects) light from the Sun.

4. Some stars (appear appears) to shine brighter during different seasons.

5. Satellites (take takes) pictures from space.

6. Scientists (study studies) the images.

7. Cartographers (use uses) the images to improve maps.

8. Astronauts (explore explores) space.

9. Mars (seem seems) to have no life.

10. An observatory (contain contains) a large, powerful telescope.

B. Match each subject noun with a verb. Match nouns 1–5 with verbs a–e and nouns 6–10 with verbs f–j.

	NOUN	VERB		NOUN	VERB
_____	1. astronauts	a. spins	_____	6. telescopes	f. flies
_____	2. stars	b. shine	_____	7. the shuttle	g. experiment
_____	3. Earth	c. space walk	_____	8. sunlight	h. magnify
_____	4. satellites	d. shoots	_____	9. a planet	i. heats
_____	5. a comet	e. orbit	_____	10. researchers	j. rotates

57. Simple Past Tense

> A verb in the **simple past tense** tells about something that happened in the past.
>
> John <u>looked</u> at stories, myths, and legends as ways to understand human beings.

A. Circle the verb that shows past tense.

1. Robinson Crusoe (land landed) on a deserted island.

2. He (see saw) that he had to provide for himself.

3. John (knows knew) that he could learn about survival from reading about Crusoe.

4. Tall tales (showed show) the American spirit.

5. Characters such as Paul Bunyan and Pecos Bill (stand stood) larger than life.

6. Myths and legends often (told tell) about imaginary characters with great accomplishments or ideas.

7. Stories about some real people, such as Daniel Boone and Davy Crockett, (become became) legends.

8. In Greek myths Zeus (rule ruled) the gods.

9. In the legend of King Arthur, the knights (sit sat) at a round table.

10. Native Americans (use used) stories about the past to teach children about their beliefs.

B. Write the past tense of each verb.

PRESENT	PAST	PRESENT	PAST
1. go	_____	6. jump	_____
2. take	_____	7. throw	_____
3. eat	_____	8. remember	_____
4. learn	_____	9. come	_____
5. buy	_____	10. read	_____

58. Future Tense with *Will*

> The word *will* is one way to express something that will take place in the future. The helping verb *will* is used with the present part of a verb to form a future tense.
>
> **I will send the invitations to our parents.**

A. Circle the words in each sentence that show the future tense.

1. Mrs. Gonzales will help you with your science project.

2. Katy will show you where the supplies are.

3. Tim will read the directions aloud.

4. Gloria will hold the frame in place.

5. You will be happy with the results.

6. We will have our science fair on Saturday.

7. Mrs. Gonzales will help us get ready.

8. Tom and Joe will put the tables in the gym.

9. Karen and Katy will make posters.

10. Ryan will hang the posters in the hall.

B. Rewrite each sentence in the future tense, using *will*.

1. The students prepare their experiments.

_____

2. Our parents arrive at two o'clock.

_____

3. Jacob takes the tickets.

_____

4. Mrs. Gonzales greets the audience.

_____

5. The judges vote for the best project.

_____

Verbs

59. Future Tense with *Going To*

> The phrase *going to* is used to express something that will happen in the future. A form of the helping verb *be* (*am, is, are, was,* or *were*) must be used in front of *going to*. *Going to* is followed by the present part of the verb.
>
> **What <u>are</u> you <u>going to</u> do on your vacation?**
> **I <u>am going to visit</u> my cousin in Boston.**

A. **Underline the words in each sentence that show the future tense.**

1. We are going to walk the Freedom Trail.
2. We are going to follow the footsteps painted on the sidewalk.
3. I am going to visit the Old North Church.
4. My cousin is going to show me Paul Revere's house.
5. I am going to see a statue of Benjamin Franklin.
6. We are going to watch the ducks in the Boston Public Garden.
7. I am going to ride on a Swan Boat there.
8. My parents are going to see the John F. Kennedy Library.
9. My dad is going to drive across the Bunker Hill Bridge.
10. My cousin is going to take me to the New England Aquarium.

B. **Rewrite each sentence in the future tense, using *going to*.**

1. We watched the baby penguins there.

   _____

2. I climbed the rock wall in the Boston Children's Museum.

   _____

3. My cousin and I attended a Red Sox game.

   _____

4. My mom bought souvenirs in Faneuil Hall.

   _____

5. We had a great time!

   _____

Verbs

Name _____

60. Present Progressive Tense

A verb in the **present progressive tense** tells what is happening now. This tense is formed with *am, is,* or *are* and the present participle.

Our class is visiting the zoo today.

Put a check in front of each sentence that uses a verb in the present progressive tense. Circle all the verbs in the present progressive tense.

_____ 1. We are staying at the zoo all day.

_____ 2. The penguin house at the zoo is attracting the most visitors.

_____ 3. The children watched the penguins eat.

_____ 4. The penguins are eating small fish.

_____ 5. A line of four penguins waddled across the ice.

_____ 6. The penguins are standing with their backs to the visitors.

_____ 7. One penguin is sleeping with its bill tucked under a flipper.

_____ 8. Another penguin is building a nest with stones.

_____ 9. The temperature was 30 degrees Fahrenheit in the penguin house.

_____ 10. Our teacher took a class picture in front of the exhibit.

_____ 11. I am buying postcards of the penguins.

_____ 12. We enjoyed our trip to the zoo.

_____ 13. The zookeeper is traveling to Antarctica to study emperor penguins.

_____ 14. Some kinds of penguins are living near the equator.

_____ 15. Our class is doing an art project about penguins.

61. Past Progressive Tense

A verb in the **past progressive tense** tells what was happening in the past. This tense is formed with *was* or *were* and the present participle.

Our whole family <u>was walking</u> through the forest.

Put a check in front of each sentence that uses a verb in the past progressive tense. Circle all the verbs in the past progressive tense.

_____ 1. The boys were watching the baseball game on television.

_____ 2. Maureen was shooting free throws at basketball practice.

_____ 3. My brothers were playing hockey.

_____ 4. James Naismith invented basketball in 1891.

_____ 5. Mom was jogging when the sun came up.

_____ 6. She was listening to music while she ran.

_____ 7. Greg was building a jigsaw puzzle after school.

_____ 8. Marbles and bowling are examples of target games.

_____ 9. Dad was going to the golf course when the rain started.

_____ 10. Their coach was calling for a time out.

_____ 11. My aunt and uncle were meeting us at the soccer match.

_____ 12. Board games use pieces moved on a flat surface.

_____ 13. The children were performing a play in the backyard.

_____ 14. Marcie was using dominoes to practice addition.

_____ 15. Our class played card games to practice multiplication facts.

62. *Is* and *Are*, *Was* and *Were*

> *Is, are, was,* and *were* are being verbs. These words do not express action. Use *is* or *was* with a singular subject.
>
> **Pottery is one kind of art.**
> **Picasso was a modern painter.**
>
> Use *are* or *were* with a plural subject.
>
> **Sculptors are famous for perfecting shape.**
> **The Impressionists were painters.**

A. Complete each sentence with *is* or *are*.

1. The photographs by Ansel Adams _____ in black and white.

2. John James Audubon _____ a world-renowned painter of birds.

3. Mobiles _____ among Alexander Calder's greatest achievements.

4. A flower _____ beautiful to Georgia O'Keeffe.

5. Mothers and babies _____ subjects of Mary Cassatt's paintings.

6. Paul Cézanne _____ often called the father of modern art.

7. Grandma Moses _____ famous for her paintings of country life.

8. Faith Ringgold's quilts _____ works of art.

9. Many drawings by M. C. Escher _____ examples of images with no beginning or end.

10. Jacob Lawrence's portraits of black leaders _____ bold and lifelike.

B. Read the following paragraph. Complete each sentence with *was* or *were*.

Leonardo da Vinci _____ a great artist, inventor, and engineer.

He _____ known for painting the *Mona Lisa*, a picture of a

woman. Flying machines and the flight of birds _____ a part of

his studies. One of his inventions _____ an underwater diving suit.

In Leonardo's lifetime many of his inventions _____ only on paper.

Verbs

63. Contractions with *Not*

A **contraction** is a short way to write some words. An apostrophe (')
marks the place where one or more letters have been left out of a word.

The word *not* is often part of a contraction. The letter *o* is left out, and
an apostrophe is used in its place. Here are some contractions with *not*.

aren't = are not   don't = do not
wasn't = was not   didn't = did not
can't = cannot   won't = will not

**A. Draw a line to match the words in Column A to the contractions
in Column B.**

COLUMN A	COLUMN B		COLUMN A	COLUMN B
1. were not	isn't		6. does not	won't
2. is not	didn't		7. are not	hadn't
3. cannot	weren't		8. was not	doesn't
4. do not	can't		9. will not	aren't
5. did not	don't		10. had not	wasn't

**B. Complete each sentence with the contraction
for the words on the left.**

cannot   1. I ___can't___ remember what a line
of longitude is.

does not   2. ___Doesn't___ a line of longitude pass
through the North Pole and the
South Pole on a globe?

was not   3. I ___wasn't___ able to find the equator
by looking at the center of the globe.

will not   4. When you travel from New York to
London, you ___won't___ cross
the equator.

are not   5. Canada and Europe ___aren't___
in the Southern Hemisphere.

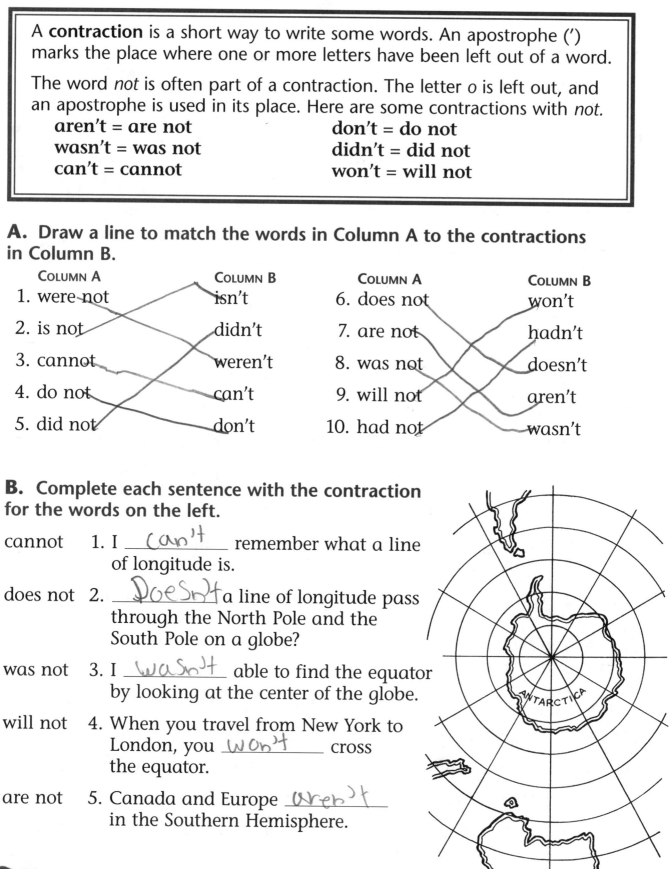

64. Reviewing Verbs

A. On the line write A for action verb or B for being verb to identify the verb in *italics* in each sentence.

_____ 1. Animals *are* an important part of the circle of life.

_____ 2. Reptiles *survive* in and out of water.

_____ 3. A cow *is* a mammal.

_____ 4. Some fish *are* able to jump out of the water.

_____ 5. Birds *build* nests in many ways.

B. Circle the correct verb for each sentence. Write *present* or *past* on the line.

_____ 6. Mary Azarian (win won) a Caldecott Medal for her illustrations in the book *Snowflake Bentley*.

_____ 7. *Salmon Summer* by Bruce McMillan (tells told) the story of a boy fishing in Alaska.

_____ 8. Yesterday we (talked talks) about the book *Martha Calling* by Susan Meddaugh.

_____ 9. The Newbery Medal winner (wrote write) the best children's book last year.

_____ 10. Every year Caldecott Medal winners (create created) the finest illustrations in children's books.

C. Write the past and the past participle of each verb.

	PAST	PAST PARTICIPLE
11. buy	_____	(had) _____
12. write	_____	(had) _____
13. sit	_____	(had) _____
14. take	_____	(had) _____
15. see	_____	(had) _____

CONTINUED

67

D. Circle the helping verb and underline the main verb in each sentence.

16. Justin is reading a timeline of air travel.

17. Ann and Mary are looking for the year of the first supersonic flight.

18. The class has found the flight of Orville and Wilbur Wright at 1903.

19. The first manned mission to the moon was flown in 1969.

20. Before the Mars rover landed, the first space shuttle had rocketed to fame in 1981.

E. Circle the verb in each sentence. On the line write **R** if the verb is regular or **I** if it is irregular.

_____ 21. Egyptians built the Great Pyramids.

_____ 22. The Maya constructed stone temples in Mexico and Central America.

_____ 23. The Chinese people felt safe behind the Great Wall of China.

_____ 24. The statue of Zeus at Olympia honored a Greek god.

_____ 25. Native American children learned to respect the land.

Try It Yourself

Write three sentences about a place you have visited. Use at least one verb that shows action, one that is in the past tense, and one that is irregular.

_____

_____

_____

Check Your Own Work

Choose a piece of writing from your portfolio, a work in progress, an assignment from another class, or a letter. Revise it, using the skills you have reviewed. This checklist will help you.

✔ Have you used a helping verb when needed?

✔ Have you spelled past tense verbs correctly, including irregular verbs?

✔ Have you used the past participle with *has, had,* or *have?*

Verbs

65. Adjectives

> **Adjectives** describe nouns. They can tell how something looks, tastes, sounds, feels, or smells. In this sentence the nouns are underlined and the adjectives are in *italics*.
>
> *Many* <u>children</u> have a *favorite* <u>author</u>.

A. Circle the adjective that describes the underlined noun.

1. Beverly Cleary is a famous <u>author</u>.
2. She writes enjoyable <u>stories</u> about children and their families.
3. Boys and girls enjoy the funny <u>tales</u> of Ramona Quimby.
4. Ramona is a delightful <u>character</u>.
5. My favorite <u>book</u> is *Ramona and Her Father*.
6. Beverly Cleary won a special <u>award</u> for that book.
7. Ramona once crowned herself with prickly <u>burrs</u>.
8. Her father worked hard to comb her messy <u>hair</u>.
9. What splendid <u>pictures</u> Ramona and her father drew.
10. They shared happy <u>days</u> together.

B. Complete each sentence with an adjective that describes the noun in *italics*.

1. Jill walked into the _____ *library*.
2. She opened the _____ *door* and went inside.
3. A _____ *librarian* helped her.
4. She directed Jill to a _____ *room*.
5. _____ *children* were in the room.
6. Some students looked at _____ *books*.
7. Jill hoped to find a _____ *book*.
8. Others listened to _____ *stories* on tape.
9. Jill walked over to the _____ *exhibit*.
10. She liked the _____ *pictures* best.

66. Adjectives Before Nouns

Most adjectives describe size, shape, color, weight, age, or other features of nouns. They are called **descriptive adjectives**. Descriptive adjectives usually come before the nouns they describe.

The <u>tall</u> man was carrying a <u>heavy</u> bag.

A. Underline the descriptive adjective in each sentence. Circle the noun that it describes.

1. Flamingos are beautiful birds.

2. They have pink feathers.

3. Flamingos often live in muddy lagoons.

4. They wade though the water on long legs.

5. Flamingos eat seeds, plants, and small animals such as crawfish.

6. They filter food from the water through their large beaks.

7. Flamingos live in huge flocks.

8. They are found in places with tropical weather.

9. Flamingos need fresh water to drink.

10. Some of them drink hot water from geysers.

B. Complete each sentence with a descriptive adjective. Underline the noun that each adjective describes.

1. Mom and I made a _____ salad for dinner.

2. I shredded some _____ lettuce.

3. Mom sliced some _____ carrots.

4. We added some _____ beets.

5. I sprinkled on some _____ cheese.

Adjectives

67. Subject Complements

Some descriptive adjectives come after being verbs such as *is, are, was,* and *were.* Those adjectives are called **subject complements.** A subject complement tells more about the subject of a sentence. In this sentence the subject is underlined and the subject complements are in *italics.*

The <u>hike</u> is *long* and *difficult.*

A. Circle the subject complement or subject complements in each sentence. Each subject is underlined.

1. The <u>trail</u> was hilly and rocky.

2. The <u>trees</u> in the forest are tall.

3. The <u>bridge</u> across the stream was wooden.

4. The <u>squirrels</u> in the tree are noisy.

5. The <u>butterflies</u> were graceful and colorful.

6. The <u>songs</u> of the birds were cheerful.

7. A <u>cloud</u> was large and dark.

8. The <u>rain</u> was cold.

9. The <u>trail</u> is slippery in the rain.

10. The <u>hikers</u> were tired after their walk.

B. Complete each sentence with an adjective from the list. Use each adjective once.

brave high clear rainy difficult

1. The mountains are _____.

2. The water in mountain streams is _____.

3. Hiking in the mountains is _____.

4. The weather at the coast is _____.

5. The climbers were _____.

Adjectives

71

68. Compound Subject Complements

Sometimes two adjectives are joined by *and, but,* or *or* after a being verb. They form a **compound subject complement.** Both adjectives tell about the subject.

The popcorn was <u>crunchy</u> and <u>salty</u>.

A. Underline the subject complements in each sentence. Circle the noun or pronoun they describe.

1. The party was fun and festive.

2. The decorations were bright and colorful.

3. The hamburgers were juicy and tasty.

4. The cider was spicy and warm.

5. The corn was hot and buttery.

6. The games were silly or tricky.

7. The costumes were funny or scary.

8. The prizes were popular and inexpensive.

9. The band was small but loud.

10. By evening I was tired and happy.

B. Complete each sentence with a compound subject complement. Choose from these adjectives.

brown	flexible	gray	Asian	sharp
curved	African	heavy	long	tall

1. Elephants are _____ and _____.

2. The two kinds of elephants are _____ and _____.

3. Their tusks are _____ and _____.

4. An elephant's trunk is _____ and _____.

5. Elephants are usually _____ or _____.

69. Adjectives That Compare

Many adjectives that compare two nouns end with *-er.*
The Mississippi River is <u>longer</u> than the Minnesota River.
Many adjectives that compare three or more nouns end with *-est.*
The <u>longest</u> river in the world is the Nile River in Africa.

A. Circle the correct adjective in parentheses.

1. The (deeper deepest) lake in the world is in Siberia.

2. The Caspian Sea is (larger largest) than Lake Superior.

3. Lake Michigan is (warmer warmest) than Lake Superior.

4. Lake Erie is (smaller smallest) than Lake Michigan.

5. Lake Ontario is the (smaller smallest) lake of the five Great Lakes.

B. Complete each pair of sentences, using the given words.

taller   tallest

1. Which is the _____ mountain in the United States?

2. This mountain is _____ than that one.

steeper   steepest

3. The trail up the mountain was _____ than he thought.

4. This section of trail is the _____ part so far.

colder   coldest

5. At what time of day is the temperature _____?

6. I was _____ in the morning than in the afternoon.

higher   highest

7. That goat has climbed _____ than we have.

8. Of all the mountain peaks, that one is the _____ peak.

harder   hardest

9. The _____ part of the hike was the climb.

10. Climbing down was _____ than I thought it would be.

Adjectives

70. More Adjectives That Compare

Adjectives that compare often end in *-er* or *-est*. Here are some spelling rules for making adjectives that compare.

If an adjective ends in *e*, drop the final *e* and add *-er* or *-est*.

wide　　　**wider**　　　**widest**

If an adjective ends in *y* following a consonant, change the *y* to *i* and add *-er* or *-est*.

happy　　**happier**　　**happiest**

If an adjective ends in a consonant that follows a vowel, double the final consonant before adding *-er* or *-est*.

hot　　　**hotter**　　　**hottest**

A. Write the correct words in the chart.

ADJECTIVE	COMPARE TWO NOUNS	COMPARE MORE THAN TWO NOUNS
1. chilly	_____	_____
2. flat	_____	_____
3. safe	_____	_____
4. big	_____	_____
5. tricky	_____	_____
6. pale	_____	_____
7. sad	_____	_____
8. tiny	_____	_____
9. large	_____	_____
10. snowy	_____	_____

B. Underline the adjective that compares in each sentence.

1. Mexico City is the largest city in North America.

2. Mexico City is bigger than New York City.

3. Boston is windier than Chicago.

4. The weather is much hotter in Tampa than in Seattle.

5. San Diego may have the nicest weather in the United States.

Adjectives

71. Irregular Adjectives That Compare

Some adjectives that compare are irregular. They are not formed by adding *-er* or *-est*. Two common irregular adjectives are *good* and *bad*.

	COMPARE TWO NOUNS	COMPARE THREE OR MORE NOUNS
good	better	best
bad	worse	worst

A. Write *good*, *better*, or *best* to complete each sentence.

1. Yesterday our team played its _____ game ever.

2. Our offense was _____ than theirs.

3. We made some really _____ plays.

4. The defense was _____ in the second half than in the first half.

5. Hank made the _____ play of the game.

B. Write *bad*, *worse*, or *worst* to complete each sentence.

1. Last night the weather reporter said, "There is no _____ weather, only bad clothes."

2. She has not been to Mount Washington, which has some of the _____ weather anywhere.

3. Mount Washington is in New Hampshire, but its weather can be as _____ as Antarctica's.

4. The wind and snow are _____ there than at most places.

5. Areas that are in mountains often have the _____ winter temperatures in the United States.

C. Complete each sentence to make it true about you.

1. My best subject is _____.

2. I am better at _____ than _____.

3. I am worst at playing _____.

4. I am good at making _____.

5. My best friend is _____.

72. Adjectives That Tell How Many

Some adjectives tell exactly how many: *first, six, eight, thirty.*
   Joel has twelve math problems left to do.
Some adjectives tell about how many: *few, several, some.*
   A few days ago we didn't have homework!

A. Circle the adjective that tells how many.
Write E if the adjective tells exactly how many.
Write A if the adjective tells about how many.

a 1. Our class decided to earn (some) money for our school.

e 2. We decided to make (fifty) bookmarks.

a 3. Supplies to make each bookmark cost a (few) cents.

e 4. We sold each bookmark for (twenty) cents.

a 5. Our profit was (several) times what we earned last year.

B. Underline the adjective that tells how many.

1. There were <u>many</u> stores in town.

2. Only <u>three</u> stores sold clothing.

3. Lisa needed a <u>few</u> new sweaters.

4. Tony wanted <u>two</u> pairs of shoes.

5. For <u>several</u> days they visited those clothing stores.

6. Lisa and Tony found <u>things</u> they wanted in the <u>second</u> store.

7. Tony's shoes cost <u>twenty</u> dollars.

8. Lisa wished the sweaters cost <u>less</u> money.

9. Lisa realized she could not buy <u>many</u> sweaters with her savings.

10. Tony had only <u>thirty-five</u> cents left after he had paid for his shoes.

73. Articles

A, an, and *the* point out nouns. They are called **articles.**

A and *an* point out any one of a group of people, places, or things. Use *a* before a word that begins with a consonant sound. Use *an* before a word that begins with a vowel sound.

I heard a bluebird.   **I saw an eagle.**

The points out a specific person, place, or thing.

The bluebird was on the branch.
I photographed the eagle as it flew by.

Circle the article in each sentence. Underline the noun that each article points out.

1. John James Audubon was a naturalist.

2. He was also an artist who painted pictures of birds.

3. The pictures that he painted are very famous.

4. Audubon was born on the island that is now called Haiti.

5. When he was 18, he moved to the commonwealth of Pennsylvania.

6. He went into business and drew pictures of birds as a hobby.

7. Later he worked full-time as a painter.

8. Audubon wanted to paint a picture of every kind of bird.

9. To do that, he studied the birds outdoors.

10. Each of his paintings is a life-sized portrait of one kind of bird.

Audubon painted birds in their natural surroundings. He helped people appreciate wildlife. Give an example of how you might show respect for wildlife.

74. Demonstrative Adjectives

> *This, that, these,* and *those* are **demonstrative adjectives.** They point out specific people, places, or things. *This* and *these* point to nouns that are near.
> **This** pond feels warm.
> *That* and *those* point to nouns that are farther away.
> **That** swamp twenty miles away is an important ecosystem.

A. **Put an X on the line before the correct answer.**

1. Which river is farther away?

    _____ This river is deep.   __X__ That river has a bridge.

2. Which lake is closer?

    _____ That lake is deep.   __X__ This lake is beautiful.

3. Which stream is farther away?

    __X__ That stream dried up.   _____ This stream is clean.

4. Which ocean is closer?

    __X__ This ocean is home to seals.   _____ That ocean is home to tuna.

5. Which wetland is closer?

    _____ That wetland is changing.   __X__ This wetland is stable.

B. **Complete each sentence with *this* or *that*.**

1. __this__ desert we are traveling through is hot.

2. Cactus grows in __that__ desert but not here.

3. Toucans live in __that__ rain forest, which is far away.

4. __this__ forest we saw in the picture yesterday is in South America.

5. Look in __that__ grassland area for any animals that might be here.

Adjectives

75. Proper Adjectives

A **proper adjective** is formed from a proper noun. A proper adjective always begins with a capital letter.

PROPER NOUN   **Have you ever been to Mexico?**
PROPER ADJECTIVE   **I like Mexican food.**

Here are some examples of proper nouns and their proper adjectives.

China	Chinese	Kenya	Kenyan
Japan	Japanese	Russia	Russian
India	Indian	France	French
Poland	Polish	Greece	Greek

A. Underline the proper adjective in each sentence.
Circle the noun it describes.

1. My aunt bought me a warm Irish sweater.

2. This cuckoo clock came from a German store.

3. I made a sandwich with ham and Swiss cheese.

4. This Brazilian music is fun to dance to.

5. An African elephant has really large ears.

B. Complete each sentence with the proper adjective for the proper noun in parentheses. Use a dictionary if you need help.

1. Spaghetti is my favorite _____ food. (Italy)

2. Many people cross the _____ border every day. (Canada)

3. Hans Christian Andersen was a _____ writer. (Denmark)

4. The museum had a collection of _____ art. (Vietnam)

5. My mom enjoys _____ coffee. (Turkey)

76. Nouns Used as Adjectives

Sometimes a noun can be used as an adjective. When two nouns are used together, the first one often acts as an adjective. It tells more about the second noun.

> We bought apples at the <u>fruit</u> stand.
> We made <u>apple</u> pie.

Circle each noun that is used as an adjective.
Underline the noun it describes.

1. In the 1800s pioneers traveled to the West in simple farm wagons.

2. The wagons were fitted with canvas tops.

3. They were filled with food, tools, clothing, furniture, and household supplies.

4. Pioneer families had to fit all of their belongings in the wagons.

5. Every day the pioneers ate a sunrise breakfast of bread and bacon before they hit the trail.

6. After walking for hours they would have a lunch break, and then they would start walking again.

7. Around 6 p.m. the settlers would put their wagons in a circle to make a livestock corral.

8. After an evening meal, everyone went to sleep.

9. By the end of the long journey, the families had worn out their shoe leather.

10. Many pioneers built themselves log cabins when the journey was over.

77. Reviewing Adjectives

A. Circle the adjective that describes each underlined noun.

1. Graceful <u>eagles</u> soared through the air.

2. Once Mali saw playful <u>lions</u> through his binoculars.

3. The orange <u>birds</u> have short <u>bills</u>.

4. Children enjoy watching garden <u>snakes</u>.

5. We think <u>donkeys</u> are stubborn.

B. Decide whether the adjective in *italics* tells exactly or about how many. Write *exactly* or *about* on the line.

___about___ 6. Kiyoshi traveled *many* miles to reach Asia.

___exactly___ 7. He visited the Great Wall of China on the *second* day of his trip.

___about___ 8. Arina knew that *numerous* islands make up the Philippines.

___about___ 9. She relaxed on an island beach for a *few* days.

___exactly___ 10. Jeb saw *six* elephants carry logs to a river in Thailand.

C. Choose the correct article for each noun. Write *a* or *an* on the line.

11. _____ mountain

12. _____ island

13. _____ volcano

14. _____ river

15. _____ inlet

16. _____ peninsula

17. _____ wetland

18. _____ acre

19. _____ earthquake

20. _____ ocean

CONTINUED

Adjectives

Adjectives

D. Circle the correct form of the word to compare the nouns in each sentence.

21. January is (**longer** longest) than February.

22. The (colder **coldest**) temperatures in the world are in Antarctica.

23. The (brighter **brightest**) day of this year was during the summer.

24. Leaves are (**prettier** prettiest) in fall than in summer.

25. Seasons are (**shorter** shortest) than years.

26. A butterfly is (**quicker** quickest) than a caterpillar.

27. Caterpillars are some of the (slower **slowest**) animals in the world.

28. A caterpillar is (**thinner** thinnest) than its cocoon.

29. The (smaller **smallest**) butterfly has a wingspan of less than one centimeter.

30. The change from caterpillar to butterfly is (**grander** grandest) than anything else!

Try It Yourself
Close your eyes and imagine that you are in a desert, rain forest, or grassland. Write three sentences, using adjectives to describe and compare the plants and animals you imagine.

_____

_____

_____

Check Your Own Work
Choose a piece of writing from your portfolio, a work in progress, an assignment from another class, or a letter. Revise it, using the skills you have reviewed. This checklist will help you.

✔ Have you correctly used an adjective that tells exactly how many or about how many?

✔ Did you use the correct form of the adjective when you were comparing two or more things?

✔ Did you use the correct demonstrative adjective to show whether nouns are near or far?

78. Adverbs

An **adverb** tells more about a verb. Some adverbs tell *when,* *where,* or *how* something happens. Many adverbs end in *-ly.*

WHEN	I flew my kite today.
WHERE	The kite flew high in the air.
HOW	I ran quickly across the field.

A. Look at each verb in *italics.* Underline the adverb that tells more about that verb.

1. Many choices you *make* today help you and others enjoy good health.

2. Germs from a sneeze *spread* easily to your hands, but you can sneeze into the crook of your arm.

3. Owen *brushes* his teeth thoroughly.

4. Rosario *washes* her hands often.

5. Good feelings are important for health, so friends who *listen* carefully help us to have good health.

6. Promise that we *will exercise* together.

7. When my brothers disagree, they *act* peacefully to solve a problem.

8. When I *speak* kindly to you, we both feel good.

9. The foods we *eat* daily should be fresh and nutritious.

10. Visit a beautiful place and *breathe* deeply.

B. Complete each sentence with an adverb from the list. Use each adverb once.

| always | downstairs | fast | patiently | there |

1. A tornado travels very __fast__ .

2. You should __alway__ listen for tornado alerts.

3. When you hear a tornado warning, go __downstairs__ to the basement.

4. Take your pets __there__ with you.

5. Wait __patiently__ until you hear the "all clear" signal.

79. Adverbs That Tell *When* or *How Often*

> **Adverbs** tell more about verbs.
> Some adverbs tell when or how often an action happens.
> **Nicholas *read* <u>yesterday</u>.**

Underline the adverbs that tell when. The verbs are in *italics*.

1. Thomas Gallaudet *was born* <u>late</u> in the year of 1787.

2. He <u>eventually</u> *wanted* to teach deaf people.

3. He <u>soon</u> *went* to France to visit schools for deaf people.

4. When he <u>finally</u> *came* home, he knew how to use sign language.

5. He *traveled* <u>frequently</u> in the United States to raise money for a school.

6. Gallaudet <u>then</u> *founded* the American Asylum for Deaf-Mutes.

7. He *worked* <u>daily</u> to make the school a success.

8. There *had been* no free public school for the deaf <u>before</u>.

9. Because of Gallaudet's efforts, deaf people in the United States <u>now</u> *can receive* education.

10. Deaf people <u>often</u> *communicate* by using sign language.

 Thomas Gallaudet's efforts improved the lives of deaf people in America. Give an example of something you could do to help someone with a disability.

Adverbs and Conjunctions

80. Adverbs That Tell *Where*

> Some adverbs tell where an action takes place.
> *Search* everywhere on the Internet.

dont Post

100%

A. Underline the adverbs that tell where. The verbs are in *italics*.

1. Do not *stand* up at the computer.

2. *Type* in a key word or topic to *start* a search.

3. *Press* down on the enter key to begin a search.

4. *Discover* useful links underneath.

5. *Scroll* forward for more text.

6. *Scroll* backward to review text.

7. *Look* away from the screen to rest your eyes.

8. *Print* out related information.

9. *Skim* and *scan* everywhere to gather information.

10. *Save* your notes here.

100%

Go to your IXL
Idify Adverbs 3rd

B. Complete each sentence with an adverb listed.
Use each adverb once.

close   inside   on   out   here

1. Beekeepers build hives ___here___ in our town.

2. Beekeeping is seldom done ___close___ to a house.

3. When beekeepers check the hives, they rarely look ___inside___.

4. A beekeeper lifts a frame ___out___ of the hive to collect the honey.

5. A bee makes only one teaspoon of honey during its
   whole life, no matter how many flowers it lands ___on___.

81. Adverbs That Tell *How*

> Some adverbs tell how an action takes place.
> **Scientists *gather* information <u>carefully</u>.**

A. Underline the adverbs that tell how. The verbs are in *italics*.

1. A zoologist in the National Zoo *observes* pandas <u>quietly</u>.

2. The information *is charted* <u>expertly</u>.

3. Zoologists *learn* about pandas <u>quickly</u>.

4. They help pandas *live* <u>contentedly</u>.

5. Feeding *is* <u>precisely</u> *monitored*.

6. The scientists <u>expertly</u> *plan* the feeding schedules.

7. For an unhappy panda, a zoologist <u>slowly</u> *changes* the environment.

8. Zoologists <u>carefully</u> *improve* the situation.

9. The zoo team <u>thoroughly</u> *evaluates* each change.

10. Pandas *munch* <u>happily</u> on bamboo.

B. Circle the verb. Write the adverb that tells how.

1. Jack carefully (emptied) his fish tank.   _carefully_

2. Nervously, the fish (swam) in a bowl.   _nervously_

3. Slowly, Jack (scrubbed) the tank clean.   _slowly_

4. He (refilled) the tank neatly.   _neatly_

5. Jack gently (placed) the fish in its tank.   _gently_

Name _____

82. More Adverbs

An **adverb** tells more about a verb. Adverbs can tell when, where, or how something happens.

WHEN	I went bird watching <u>yesterday</u>.
WHERE	There is a bird sanctuary <u>nearby</u>.
HOW	Most birds fly <u>quickly</u>.

A. Underline the adverb in each sentence. Does it tell **when, where, or how?** Write *when, where,* or *how* on the line.

_100%_

where 1. People <u>everywhere</u> like to watch birds.

when 2. Bird watchers get up <u>early</u>.

where 3. They go <u>outside</u> and visit a field or forest.

How 4 They walk <u>quietly</u>.

how 5. They listen <u>carefully</u> for any sounds.

where 6. They look <u>around</u>, checking for any movement.

how 7. They wait <u>patiently</u> to see different birds.

when 8. They try <u>never</u> to frighten the birds.

When 9. Bird watchers <u>often</u> keep lists of the birds they see.

When 10. <u>Sometimes</u> they take pictures of the birds.

B. Complete each sentence to make it true about you. Use an adverb that tells **when, where,** or **how.** Choose adverbs from the list or use your own ideas.

_100%_

| always | ~~fast~~ | ~~never~~ | ~~often~~ | ~~slowly~~ | untidily |
| carefully | ~~inside~~ | noisily | outdoors | sometimes | upstairs |

when   1. I ___never___ do my homework on time.

how   2. I eat ___fast___.

where   3. I like to play games ___inside___.

how   4. I do my math problems ___slowly___.

when   5. In the evening I ___often___ play video games.

83. Negatives

A negative idea is formed in several ways. You can add *not* to the verb. You can add *not* as part of a contraction: *didn't, wasn't, can't.* You can add *never* before the verb. Because *not* and *never* tell about verbs, they are adverbs.

Casey is <u>not</u> careless.
She <u>doesn't</u> ride her bike without a helmet.
She <u>never</u> leaves her bike in the driveway.

Be careful to use only one negative word in a sentence.

INCORRECT	**She <u>doesn't</u> <u>never</u> forget to signal.**
CORRECT	**She <u>doesn't</u> forget to signal.**
CORRECT	**She <u>never</u> forgets to signal.**

A. Underline the negative word in each sentence.

1. The experiment <u>wasn't</u> easy to do.

2. We had <u>never</u> tried to make paper before.

3. We did <u>not</u> know how to begin.

4. The instructions <u>weren't</u> clear.

5. We <u>didn't</u> know it would make such a mess.

B. Find the sentences that are incorrect. Write them correctly. Some of the sentences are correct.

1. My cousin won't play outside when it's cold.

   _____

2. He doesn't ~~never~~ ice skate.

   He doesn't ice skate.

3. He can't ski.

   _____

4. He ~~does not~~ never makes snowmen.

   He never makes snowmen.

5. He isn't ~~never~~ happy in the winter.

   He isn't happy in the winter.

84. *Good* and *Well*

> *Good* is an **adjective** that describes a noun.
>   **A good symbol is easy to recognize.**
> *Well* is an **adverb** that tells about verbs.
>   **Numbers are symbols that serve us well.**

Circle the correct word in parentheses.

1. (Good Well) signs tell people when to use caution.

2. Roads near schools should be marked (good well).

3. Stop signs are (good well) for safety.

4. It is (good well) to know that blue road signs offer information.

5. A picture with a red slash through it is a (good well) way to show that something is not allowed.

6. The poison symbol is a (good well) reminder to keep something out of the reach of children.

7. The color red works (good well) to warn us of danger.

8. People who do not speak the same language can communicate (good well) by using symbols.

9. The eagle is a (good well) symbol for our country.

10. Chris is (good well) at looking for a recycling symbol on cans.

11. Sign language works (good well) for many deaf people.

12. Musical notes are (good well) symbols for recording music.

13. Morse Code was once (good well) for communicating a message.

14. (Good Well) secret codes can be hard to decode.

15. A handshake is a (good well) sign of hello or good-bye.

85. *To*, *Too*, and *Two*

> *To* tells where, or it means "until."
>
> **Mrs. Lauer's class took a trip <u>to</u> the forest preserve.**
>
> *Too* means "also" or "more than enough."
>
> **Many parents went on the trip <u>too</u>.**
>
> *Two* means "the number 2."
>
> **The class was at the forest preserve for <u>two</u> hours.**

A. Circle *to*, *too*, or *two* to correctly complete each sentence.

1. One group went (to too two) the playground and collected trash.

2. A different group started working at 10 minutes (to too two) nine.

3. The parents helped with the cleanup (to too two).

4. Each group collected (to too two) bags of trash.

5. One bag of trash was (to too two) heavy.

6. Everyone went (to too two) the picnic area for lunch.

7. Parents brought (to too two) sandwiches for each child.

8. The class went (to too two) the river bank after lunch.

9. While at the preserve, Rosi saw (to too two) cardinals.

10. Let's clean up the school playground (to too two)!

B. Complete each sentence with the word *to*, *too*, or *two*.

1. Air and water are _____ natural resources.

2. Soil is a natural resource _____.

3. Trash that is not recycled is taken _____ a landfill.

4. Recycling and reusing are _____ ways that natural resources can be protected.

5. Leaves and grass clippings can be taken _____ a compost center.

Name _____

86. *Their* and *There*

Their tells who owns something. *Their* is an adjective.

César Chávez and his family picked fruit to earn <u>their</u> money.

There usually means "in that place." *There* is an adverb.

They lived <u>there</u>.

Complete each sentence with *there* or *their*.

1. Businesspeople who own large farms need people to work _____.

2. César Chávez saw a need for better conditions for those migrant workers who worked _____.

3. Traveling workers pick fruit and vegetables for _____ wages.

4. Chávez worked to improve _____ working conditions.

5. _____ pay was too low for the hours they worked.

6. He protested the use of pesticides that poisoned the workers and _____ children.

7. In California and Arizona he went without eating food for days to call attention to _____ cause.

8. Many groups _____ and in other states supported his work.

9. He spent his money to organize workers _____ on the farms.

10. Chávez created the United Farm Workers to work toward improving _____ wages and other benefits.

César Chávez continued his efforts to make sure migrant workers were given their rights. Give an example of how you kept on working to complete a difficult task.

87. Coordinating Conjunctions

A **coordinating conjunction** joins two words or groups of words. The words *and, but,* and *or* are coordinating conjunctions.

AND   Cows *and* chickens are farm animals.
BUT   Cows are large *but* gentle.
OR   Chickens are raised for eggs *or* for meat.

A. Circle the coordinating conjunction in each sentence. Underline the words or groups of words the coordinating conjunction joins.

1. Fruits and vegetables are grown on farms.

2. Some farmers grow wheat or soybeans.

3. Most farmers don't work with horses or with oxen.

4. Now they have tractors and harvesters.

5. Their equipment is expensive but necessary.

B. Write the coordinating conjunction that makes sense in each sentence.

   and   **but**   **or**

1. Animals are kept in barns _____ in pens.

2. Farmers feed _____ water their animals.

3. Farmers milk cows with machines _____ by hand.

4. Cheese _____ ice cream are made from milk.

5. A farmer's job is difficult _____ rewarding.

Name _____

88. Reviewing Adverbs

A. Circle the adverbs. The verbs are in *italics*.

1. The people from New York *waved* wildly at the passing parade.
2. Marching bands from Iowa *played* well.
3. The florist *displayed* the colorful flowers beautifully.
4. Huge balloons *soared* grandly on long strings.
5. Expert riders *groomed* the parade horses neatly.

B. Circle the correct adverb in parentheses.

6. (Tomorrow Yesterday) I met an author at the mall.
7. The author Christine McDonnell has (early often) visited bookstores.
8. I have (already ever) read several of her books.
9. Our teacher (sometimes early) shares her stories with us.
10. Mrs. Hughes read *Toad Food and Measle Soup* (today tomorrow).

C. Circle the adverbs. The verbs are in *italics*.

11. Please *carry* the groceries inside.
12. The bags *tumbled* down from the table.
13. *Take* the shampoo upstairs.
14. The phone bill *is* near.
15. We *looked* everywhere for the lost car keys.

D. Circle each adverb. On the line write if it tells *when, where,* or *how.*

how 16. Local produce is packaged loosely.

Where 17. Fresh tomatoes are here.

where 18. Farmers depend on selling crops locally.

how 19. People buy fresh vegetables carefully.

when 20. Stores prefer to stock fresh fruit daily.

CONTINUED

Adverbs and Conjunctions

E. Complete each sentence with *good* or *well*. 100%

21. Consumers must make _good_ choices.

22. _Good_ shoppers consider the quality and the cost of an item.

23. Products from other countries often sell _well_ if similar products are not made locally.

24. _Good_ products made locally can be sold overseas.

25. A product that is made _well_ can be the best deal.

100%

F. Circle the coordinating conjunction in each sentence. Underline the words or groups of words the coordinating conjunction joins.

26. Turtles live in water that is salty or fresh.

27. They use flippers or feet to swim.

28. Not every turtle can pull in its head and legs.

29. Turtles eat plants and insects.

30. Turtles have skin that is tough-looking but sensitive.

Try It Yourself
Describe how to make a sandwich in three or more steps. Use adverbs to explain when, where, and how you do each step.

_____

_____

_____

_____

Check Your Own Work
Choose a piece of writing from your portfolio, a work in progress, an assignment from another class, or a letter. Revise it, using the skills you have reviewed. This checklist will help you.

✔ Have you used adverbs that tell *when, where,* or *how?*

✔ Have you used *good* as an adjective and *well* as an adverb?

Name _____

89. End Punctuation

A sentence that tells something ends with a **period**.
> The sun is a star.

A sentence that asks a question ends with a **question mark**.
> How hot is the sun?

A sentence that expresses strong or sudden feeling ends with an **exclamation point**.
> Wow, that's hot!

Place the correct mark of punctuation at the end of each sentence. On the line write S if the sentence is a statement, Q if it is a question, or E if it is an exclamation.

S   1. Plants use energy from the sun.

S   2. Sunspots are dark patches on the sun.

Q   3. How do animals use the sun?

E   4. The eclipse was incredible!

S   5. Stars are hot balls of gas.

S   6. Planets are not as hot as the sun.

Q   7. Why do planets orbit the sun?

S   8. Asteroids also orbit the sun.

S   9. Telescopes help us see objects in space.

Q 10. What makes up the tail of a comet?

S 11. Astronomers are scientists who study planets.

Q 12. Did you know they also study asteroids and meteors?

S 13. There is much to discover about our solar system.

E 14. Astronomers are amazing!

S 15. I want to become one.

90. Capital Letters—Part I

The first word of a sentence always begins with a capital letter.

A disaster supply kit is important to own, even though it may never be used.

Names of people and pets begin with a capital letter.

Catherine   Rover

Names of streets, cities, states, and countries begin with capital letters.

First Avenue   Boston   Texas   Mexico

The proofreading mark (≡) is used under a letter to show that it should be capitalized.

portland, oregon, gets about 40 inches of rain each year.

A. Use the proofreading symbol (≡) to show which letters should be capitalized.

1. mexico has many earthquakes.
2. raquel's pet, blanco, was frightened in the last quake.
3. the buildings on first street were damaged.
4. people in california prepare for earthquakes.
5. india has also seen natural disasters.
6. rosina once survived a great storm in bombay, india.
7. many people in china have lived through floods.
8. ching lee saw floods in nanjing, china.
9. he now lives on university drive in fargo.
10. there he must deal with north dakota's blizzards.

B. Use the proofreading symbol (≡) to show which letters should be capitalized.

El Niño is a warm current of water in the pacific ocean. it affects the weather from the united states to south africa. El Niño might cause indira thali's family in madras, india, to live through drought and juan ruiz's home in lima, peru, to flood.

91. Capital Letters—Part II

Days of the week and months of the year begin with capital letters.
Tuesday   **August**

Holidays begin with capital letters.
Kwanzaa   **St. Patrick's Day**

A. Use the proofreading symbol (≡) to show which letters should be capitalized.

1. independence day is celebrated on july 4.

2. The parade is scheduled for saturday.

3. Is your vacation in july or august?

4. Does every state celebrate presidents' day?

5. Do we celebrate new year's day on january 1?

6. I have a dentist appointment thursday afternoon.

7. memorial day is celebrated in may.

8. My brother washes the dishes every monday and wednesday.

9. martin luther king, jr., day is a january holiday.

10. Costumes for halloween are in the stores in october.

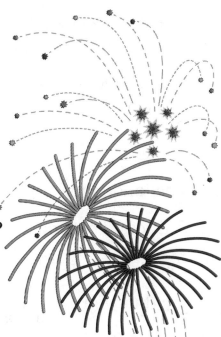

B. Complete each sentence with a holiday, day of the week, or month of the year.

day   1. _____ comes right after Wednesday.

month   2. Labor Day is in _____.

holiday   3. In November we get two days off from
                school for _____.

month   4. Valentine's Day is celebrated in _____.

day   5. _____ is the last school day of the week.

Name _____

92. Capital Letters—Part III

> Names of buildings and bridges begin with capital letters.
> **Empire State Building   Golden Gate Bridge**
> The personal pronoun *I* is a capital letter.
> **My neighbor and I will visit Texas.**

A. Use the proofreading symbol (≡) to show which letters should be capitalized.

1. You will find the library of congress in Washington, D.C.

2. The royal gorge bridge in Colorado is the world's highest bridge.

3. The eiffel tower is located in Paris, France.

4. The london tower bridge spans the Thames River in England.

5. Seth and i walked across the golden gate bridge.

6. the visitors enjoyed the art institute of Chicago.

7. my dad works at the sears tower.

8. George Washington did not live in the white house because it was being built when he was president.

9. The betsy ross bridge crosses the Delaware River.

10. This summer i will visit epcot center.

B. Use the proofreading symbol (≡) to show which letters should be capitalized.

bob and i went sightseeing in boston. we saw the famous faneuil hall. later bob and i walked across the longfellow bridge, which crosses the charles river. we then visited the john f. kennedy library. boston is certainly an exciting city in massachusetts.

Name _____

93. Abbreviations

An **abbreviation** is a short form of a word. Abbreviations for addresses begin with capital letters and usually end with periods.

    Street   St.   Place   Pl.

Abbreviations for units of measure do not begin with capital letters.

    foot   ft.   inch   in.

A. Write the abbreviation for each underlined word. Use the list below.

Blvd.   Rd.   Dr.   Ave.   Apt.
Ln.   N.   St.   W.   Pkwy.

1. Seventh Avenue _Ave._
2. Lincoln Parkway _Pkwy._
3. North Elm Street _N._
4. Addison Boulevard _Blvd._
5. Lakeview Drive _Dr._
6. Miller Road _Rd._
7. Montgomery Lane _Ln._
8. Apartment 3B _Apt._
9. Orange Street _St._
10. West Ott Road _W._

B. Write the unit of measure for each abbreviation. Use the list below.

quart pound inch pint second
mile yard gallon minute ounce

1. oz. _ounce_
2. sec. _second_
3. in. _inch_
4. qt. _quart_
5. gal. _gallon_
6. min. _minute_
7. pt. _pint_
8. mi. _mile_
9. lb. _pound_
10. yd. _yard_

Punctuation, Capitalization, Abbreviations

99

Name _____

94. More Abbreviations

Days of the week and some months of the year can be abbreviated.

MONTHS *May, June,* and *July* do not have abbreviations.
September is abbreviated using the first four letters of the word.
The rest of the months use the first three letters of each word as the abbreviation.

DAYS *Tuesday* is abbreviated using the first four letters of the word.
Thursday is abbreviated using the first five letters of the word.
The rest of the days use the first three letters of each word as the abbreviation.

A. Write the abbreviation for each month that has an abbreviation.

1. April _____ APR.

2. February _____ FEB.

3. November _____ NOV.

4. January _____ JAN.

5. June _____ JUN.

6. March _____ MAR

7. July _____ JUL

8. September _____ SEP

9. October _____ OCT

10. December _____ DEC

B. Write the correct day of the week on the line. In parentheses write the abbreviation.

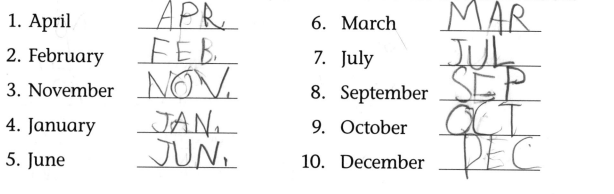

1. The day that comes in the middle of the
school week is _Wednesday_(_WED_).

2. The day before that is _Tuesday_(_TUES_).

3. The last day of the school week
is _Friday_ (_FRI_).

4. The day after that is _Saterday_(_SAT_).

5. The first day of the school week is _monday_(_mo_).

95. Titles and Initials

> Titles and names can also be abbreviated.
> *Mr.* is an abbreviated title for a man.
> *Ms.* and *Mrs.* are abbreviated titles for a woman.
> ### Doctor Roger John Kugel   Dr. R. J. Kugel

A. Match the words in Column A with the abbreviations in Column B.
Some letters will be used twice.

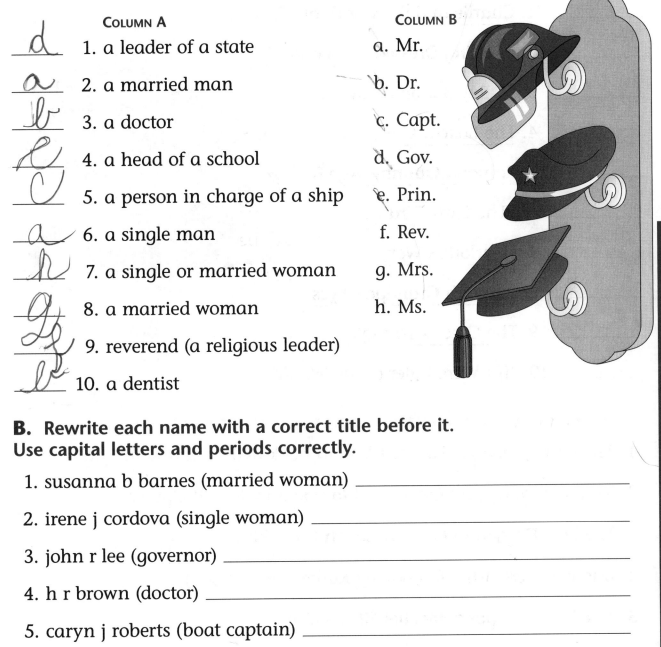

	COLUMN A	COLUMN B
d	1. a leader of a state	a. Mr.
a	2. a married man	b. Dr.
b	3. a doctor	c. Capt.
e	4. a head of a school	d. Gov.
c	5. a person in charge of a ship	e. Prin.
a	6. a single man	f. Rev.
h	7. a single or married woman	g. Mrs.
g	8. a married woman	h. Ms.
f	9. reverend (a religious leader)	
b	10. a dentist	

B. Rewrite each name with a correct title before it.
Use capital letters and periods correctly.

1. susanna b barnes (married woman) _____

2. irene j cordova (single woman) _____

3. john r lee (governor) _____

4. h r brown (doctor) _____

5. caryn j roberts (boat captain) _____

96. Titles of Books and Poems

Titles of books are underlined when handwritten.

A River Ran Wild by Lynne Cherry

Titles of poems have quotation marks around them.

"An Elephant Is Hard to Hide" by Jack Prelutsky

A. Write on the line whether each title is for a book or poem.

_____ 1. Charlie and the Chocolate Factory

_____ 2. "Getting Dressed for School"

_____ 3. "A Bug Sat on a Silver Flower"

_____ 4. The Boxcar Children

_____ 5. Ramona Quimby, Age 8

_____ 6. "The Early Bird"

_____ 7. Charlotte's Web

_____ 8. Through Grandpa's Eyes

_____ 9. The Greedy Triangle

_____ 10. "If I Were Ruler of the World"

B. Underline or place quotation marks where necessary.

1. The Best Christmas Pageant Ever (a book by Barbara Robinson)

2. An Early Worm Got Out of Bed (a poem by Jack Prelutsky)

3. The Last Dragon (a book by Susan Miho Nunes)

4. Bridge to Terabithia (a book by Katherine Paterson)

5. Tree House (a poem by Shel Silverstein)

97. More Titles of Books and Poems

Each important word in a title begins with a capital letter. The first word and the last word of a title always begin with a capital letter. A short word such as *of, to, for, a, an,* or *the* is not capitalized unless it is the first or last word in the title.

The Spy on Third (book)
"And the Green Grass Grew All Around" (poem)

A. Rewrite the titles, using capital letters where needed. Write whether each is a book or a poem.

_____ 1. chang and the bamboo flute by Elizabeth Starr Hill.

_____

_____ 2. ben and me by Robert Lawson

_____

_____ 3. "if once you have slept on an island" by Rachel Field

_____

_____ 4. "every time i climb a tree" by David McCord

_____

_____ 5. elisa in the middle by Johanna Hurwitz

_____

B. Write each title correctly.

1. the owl and the pussycat (poem)

_____

2. beans on the roof (book)

_____

3. clever polly and the stupid wolf (book)

_____

4. the midnight ride of paul revere (poem)

_____

5. when i was young in the mountains (book)

_____

Punctuation, Capitalization, Abbreviations

98. Commas in a Series

> Three or more words or groups of words of the same kind written one after another are called a **series.** Often parts of the series are connected by the coordinating conjunction *and* or *or.* Commas are used to separate words in a series.
>
> **Light, heat, and sound are forms of energy.**
> **Did a person, an animal, or a thing make that sound?**

Rewrite each sentence. Add commas to separate the items in series.

1. Trucks planes and motorcycles make loud sounds.

   _____

2. Dripping rain purring cats and blowing leaves make soft sounds.

   _____

3. A bird a kitten or a small bell makes a high sound.

   _____

4. Lions cows and bears make low sounds.

   _____

5. People can make sounds by shaking hitting or blowing into musical instruments.

   _____

6. We shake maracas rattles and tambourines to make sounds.

   _____

7. You can make sounds by hitting a drum a triangle or a gong.

   _____

8. They blow into harmonicas recorders and horns to make sounds.

   _____

9. People also use their lips teeth and tongues to make sounds.

   _____

10. The outer ear the eardrum and the inner ear help us to hear sounds.

    _____

99. Commas in Direct Address

Speaking directly to a person and using that person's name is called **direct address.** Commas are used to separate the name of the person spoken to from the rest of the sentence.

Turn on the light, Thomas Edison.
Please, Louis Braille, read these dots.

Insert one or more commas to separate the name of the person spoken to from the rest of the sentence.

1. Take a picture George Eastman.

2. Thanks for the stuffed toy Ms. Steiff.

3. Launch the rocket Robert Goddard.

4. Mary Anderson wipe the windshield.

5. Play ball Alexander Cartwright!

6. Benjamin Banneker water the crops.

7. Find the computer bug Grace Hopper.

8. Check out a library book Melvil Dewey.

9. Laszlo Biro please hand me that ballpoint pen.

10. These books Mr. Gutenberg are printed beautifully.

11. Please answer the phone Alexander Graham Bell.

12. Helicopters Igor Sikorsky are amazing flying machines.

13. Benjamin Franklin let's go to the public library.

14. The light bulb Joseph Swan is a remarkable invention.

15. Let's make more of everything Mr. Ford.

16. Find hundreds of uses for peanuts George Washington Carver.

17. Inventors Jean are important to all of us.

18. Do you realize Andy what Eli Whitney accomplished?

19. Kathleen what is your favorite invention?

20. Name something Mr. Hartfield that you could not do if there were no inventors.

100. Commas in Compound Sentences

A comma is used when two short sentences are combined into one longer sentence. This longer sentence is called a **compound sentence.** To make a compound sentence, use a comma followed by *and, but,* or *or.*

> **We get together for Thanksgiving, and we cook a big meal.**
> **I like other holidays, but Thanksgiving is my favorite.**
> **We will watch a football game, or we will go for a walk.**

Combine each pair of sentences into a compound sentence. Use a comma and *and, but,* or *or.*

1. Matt made the stuffing. Allison put it into the turkey.

   _____

2. Chris whipped the potatoes. They were still lumpy.

   _____

3. Elizabeth set the table. Jason arranged the flowers.

   _____

4. Sylvia peeled the onions. She cooked them in cream.

   _____

5. Before dinner we might watch a video. We might play outdoors.

   _____

6. Katie wanted to slice the carrots. She couldn't find a knife.

   _____

7. Aaron made the salad. Ann made the salad dressing.

   _____

8. Nicky called us to dinner. I didn't hear her at first.

   _____

9. The dinner was delicious. Everyone ate a lot.

   _____

10. We'll eat the leftovers later. We'll save them for tomorrow.

   _____

101. Apostrophes

An **apostrophe** is a punctuation mark. An apostrophe is used to form the possessive of a noun.

> **The boy has a hat. The boy's hat is blue.**
> **The girls have hats. The girls' hats are red.**
> **The women have hats. The women's hats are yellow.**

An apostrophe is used to replace letters left out in a contraction.
> **He is not coming because he cannot find his hat.**
> **He isn't coming because he can't find his hat.**

Rewrite each sentence. Add apostrophes where necessary.

1. Carlas homework isn't done.

   Carlas homework

2. The childrens lunches aren't ready.

   The children lunches aren't ready.

3. The two dogs weren't fed.

   The two dog's weren't

4. Both dogs collars were missing.

   Both dog's collars were missing

5. Dads toast wasn't hot.

   Dad's toast wasn't hot.

6. Mom couldn't unzip the babies diaper bags.

   Mom couldn't unzip the babies diaper bags

7. My three brothers shoes shouldn't be on the stairs.

   My three brother's shoes shouldn't be on the stairs.

8. Henry can't find Milton's jacket.

   Henry can't find Milton's jacket.

9. My familys day didn't start out well.

   My families day didn't start out well.

10. I hope tomorrow won't be like today.

    I hope tomorrow won't be like today.

102. Addresses

In an address capitalize the first letter of every word and abbreviation. Capitalize both letters of a state abbreviation. A comma separates the city and the state, but there is no comma between the state abbreviation and the ZIP Code. If there is an apartment, suite, or floor number, it is separated from the rest of the address by a comma.

Ms. Karen Briggs　　　　　**Dr. Charles Drew**
231 S. Banks St., Apt. 14　　**62 Hampton Rd., Suite 6A**
Columbus, OH 43203　　　　**Alexandria, VA 39532**

Rewrite each address, using capital letters and commas where needed.

1. mr. oscar perez

   2641 tijeras st.

   beaumont TX 77707

2. mrs. clair pinkney

   328 w. broad st. apt. 6C

   spokane WA 99205

3. dr. laura lin

   33 oakley rd. suite 12

   bangor ME 04401

4. gov. hector ryan

   632 peach st.

   atlanta GA 30303

5. capt. ann rosen

   4656 crescent court

   reno NV 89506

103. Direct Quotations

> A **direct quotation** contains the exact words of a person. In a quotation a comma is used to separate what is said from the rest of the sentence. Quotation marks are placed before and after the words of a speaker.
>
> > Pam said, "There were 13 original colonies."
> > "You are correct," stated the quizmaster.

A. Put commas and quotation marks in the correct places.

1. Connecticut was one of the 13 colonies announced the tour guide.

2. The Gullah people are important to American history explained Mr. Jolie.

3. Ms. Garcia said John Jay worked with George Washington.

4. That is the Liberty Bell whispered a tourist.

5. The colonists opposed the king she said.

B. Rewrite each sentence, using quotation marks, commas, and capital letters.

1. Let's visit Colonial Williamsburg begged the class.

   _____

2. Ms. scadron said we can see how people once lived in virginia.

   _____

3. joseph continued they have a fife-and-drum parade.

   _____

4. We can eat colonial food replied arthur.

   _____

5. Then let's go to Yorktown suggested michelle.

   _____

104. More Direct Quotations

> Sometimes the exact words of a speaker ask a question or express strong feeling.
> Use a question mark when the exact words are a question.
> Use an exclamation point when the exact words are an exclamation. The question mark and the exclamation point come before the end quotation marks in direct quotations.
>
> **"What's the state bird of Illinois?" asked Sandy.**
> **"It's a cardinal!" exclaimed her cousin.**

Put question marks and exclamation points in the correct places. Then add quotation marks to complete the sentences.

1. Did you know that California has a state animal asked Lily.

2. It's the California Grizzly Bear yelled Eliza.

3. Look at all the bluebonnets exclaimed Mark.

4. Why are there so many bluebonnets in Texas asked Shoshanna.

5. Evan asked Is the dogwood of Virginia a flower or a tree

6. It's both shouted Pia.

7. What do you think the state beverage is in Florida asked Maria.

8. Ned shouted Orange juice, of course

9. Alaska has fine salmon cried the warden.

10. Is it the state fish asked the tourist.

11. Would you like to visit the Empire State Building asked the guide.

12. You are lucky to live near Mount Rushmore yelled Marlene.

13. Let's swim in the Great Salt Lake shouted Natalia.

14. The wind is howling across the plains shrieked Linda.

15. Kenisha asked Have you been to Niagara Falls

105. Reviewing Punctuation, Capitalization, and Abbreviations

A. Write the abbreviation for each word.

1.	Sunday	Sun.	11.	Thursday	Thur.
2.	Friday	Fri.	12.	Tuesday	Tue.
3.	Saturday	Sat.	13.	yard	yrd.
4.	Wednesday	Wed.	14.	gallon	gal.
5.	Monday	Mon.	15.	Boulevard	Blvd.
6.	April	Apr.	16.	December	Dec.
7.	August	Aug.	17.	doctor	Dr.
8.	September	Sept.	18.	married woman	Mrs.
9.	October	Oct.	19.	single or married woman	Ms.
10.	November	Nov.	20.	single or married man	Mr.

B. Write the proofreading symbol (≡) under the letters that should be capitalized.

21. mary lives at 3040 wellington street.

22. Our family has a picnic on memorial day.

23. we saw the oakland bay bridge in the distance.

24. The empire state building is in new york city.

25. ann moved to chicago, illinois.

C. Put commas in the correct places and put the correct mark of punctuation at the end of each sentence.

26. Is this your music Ludwig von Beethoven

27. Georgia O'Keeffe what gorgeous flowers you paint

28. Will you blow the trumpet Louis Armstrong

29. Balance your mobile Alexander Calder

30. Wolfgang Amadeus Mozart your music is magnificent

Name _____

D. Put commas, quotation marks, question marks, and exclamation points in the correct places.

31. Mrs. Carr asked Do you like popcorn

32. Dennis exclaimed It's my favorite snack

33. Did you know that most popcorn is grown in the Midwest asked Mrs. Carr.

34. Ohio Iowa Illinois and Indiana are all popcorn producers added Jeff.

35. Jeanne shouted Popcorn is ready

Try It Yourself
What famous person in history do you wish you could speak with on the telephone? Write a question you would ask and how the person might reply. Use quotation marks, commas, question marks, and exclamation points correctly.

_____

_____

_____

_____

_____

Check Your Own Work
Choose a piece of writing from your portfolio, a work in progress, an assignment from another class, or a letter. Revise it, using the skills you have reviewed. This checklist will help you.

✔ Do you end each sentence with the correct punctuation mark?

✔ Have you followed the rules for commas?

✔ Did you use quotation marks before and after speakers' words?

✔ Have you capitalized all proper nouns?

✔ Have you spelled abbreviations correctly?

106. Subjects and Predicates

A **diagram** is a drawing that shows how the parts of a sentence go together. There is no punctuation in a diagram of a sentence.

SENTENCE: **Fish swim.**

Start the diagram by drawing a horizontal line (a line that goes across). Find the verb in the sentence and write it on the right side of the line. Find the subject and write it in front of the verb. Draw a vertical line (a line that goes up and down) between the subject and the verb. The vertical line should cut through the horizontal line.

Fish	swim

Diagram each of these sentences.

1. Babies cry.

2. Linda shouted.

3. We won.

4. Bees buzz.

CONTINUED

5. Jake ran.

6. She cooks.

7. Eagles fly.

8. Dad sang.

9. Kittens purr.

10. I skated.

107. Possessives

In a diagram a possessive noun is written on a slanted line under the noun it goes with. The possessive adjectives *my, your, his, her, its, our,* and *their* are diagrammed the same way.

SENTENCE: **Karen's puppy wiggled.**

~~puppy~~ | ~~wiggled~~
Karen's

Diagram each of these sentences.

1. My balloon burst.

2. Jack's roses bloomed.

3. Our roof leaks.

Diagramming

CONTINUED

4. Mom's canary sings.

5. Their team lost.

6. Maya's phone rang.

7. His kite flew.

8. Rabbits' ears twitch.

108. Adjectives

In a diagram an adjective is written on a slanted line under the noun it tells about.

SENTENCE: **Shiny trumpets blared.**

Diagram each of these sentences.

1. Many stars twinkled.

2. Hungry wolves prowl.

3. Funny things happened.

4. The wind blew.

CONTINUED

Diagramming

5. Big waves crashed.

6. Cool rain fell.

7. Angry bees sting.

8. The children played.

9. Little chicks peeped.

10. Two puppies slept.

109. Adverbs

In a diagram an adverb is written on a slanted line under the verb it tells about.

SENTENCE: **The crowd cheered loudly.**

Diagram each of these sentences.

1. Our team played well.

2. The bird chirped sweetly.

3. Good cooks measure carefully.

4. Monkeys chatter noisily.

CONTINUED

119

5. Monica's class worked hard.

6. The contest ends tomorrow.

7. The train raced forward.

8. My mother sews beautifully.

9. Bill's horse jumped gracefully.

10. The teakettle whistles loudly.

110. Adjectives as Complements

In a diagram an adjective used as a subject complement is written on the horizontal line to the right of the verb. A slanted line that points back at the subject separates the adjective from the verb.

SENTENCE: **My dad is tall.**

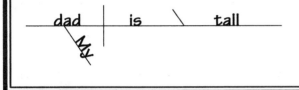

Diagram each of these sentences.

1. The soup is delicious.

2. That game was easy.

3. Tom's band is terrific.

4. The room was dark.

CONTINUED

Diagramming

5. Their song was wonderful.

6. The beach was empty.

7. The sand was hot.

8. Jesse's skateboard is new.

9. My cousins are friendly.

10. Some storms are dangerous.

111. Compound Subjects

In a diagram each subject in a compound subject goes on a separate horizontal line. A dashed line for the conjunction connects the subject lines.

SENTENCE: **Kittens and puppies are cute.**

Diagram each of these sentences.

1. Mark and Nina swim well.

2. Barry and I ran fast.

3. Plums and peaches are sweet.

4. Mom and Dad worked hard.

Diagramming

5. Ana and Diego are tired.

6. Lions and cheetahs run quickly.

7. She and Toby were happy.

8. Cars and trucks stopped nearby.

9. Carol and Ned sang loudly.

10. Fritz and Sandy were proud.

Name _____

112. Compound Predicates

In a diagram each verb in a compound predicate goes on a separate horizontal line. A dashed line for the conjunction connects the simple predicates.

SENTENCE: **My brother rides and ropes.**

Diagram each of these sentences.

1. Corrine's hamster eats and plays.

2. Careful writers plan and edit.

3. The audience whistled and clapped.

CONTINUED

4. Loud thunder cracked and boomed.

5. The player shoots and scores.

6. Leland's mother draws and paints.

7. The dancer tripped and fell.

8. Our teacher jokes and laughs.

113. Compound Complements

In a diagram each adjective in a compound subject complement goes on a separate horizontal line. A dashed line for the conjunction connects the subject complements.

SENTENCE: The children were tired but happy.

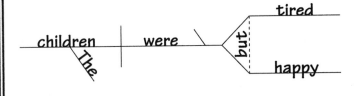

Diagram each of these sentences.

1. This mystery is funny and exciting.

2. Bella's aunt is tall and thin.

3. The parade was long and colorful.

4. His bike is old and rusty.

Diagramming

5. The pizza was hot and spicy.

6. Kevin's dog was filthy but unhurt.

7. The game was long and boring.

8. Their boat was green and blue.

9. The salad was tasty and nutritious.

10. My ferret is cute and playful.

114. Compound Sentences

To diagram a compound sentence, diagram each sentence separately, one above the other. Connect the sentences with a dashed line at the left of the sentences. Write the conjunction on the dashed line.

SENTENCE: **My brother walked slowly, but I ran.**

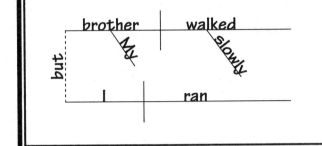

Diagram each of these sentences.

1. The cake is delicious, but the milk is sour.

2. The game was exciting, and we won easily.

3. The rain stopped, and the children ran outside.

Diagramming

4. The woods were quiet, and everyone slept soundly.

5. My brother works hard, but my sister is lazy.

6. The lion roared, and the clown ran away.

7. The movie was scary, and Melanie screamed.

8. The water was warm, and Jacob jumped in.

115. Diagramming Practice

In a diagram, the subject, the verb, and the subject complement go on the horizontal line. Possessives, adjectives, and adverbs go on slanted lines under the words they tell about.

SENTENCE: **My uncle was angry yesterday.**

```
  uncle  |  was  \  angry
      \        \
       My        yesterday
```

Diagram each of these sentences.

1. Jen's painting is beautiful.

2. The ice melted quickly.

3. Funny clowns walked backward.

4. Her movements were graceful.

Diagramming

5. Old cars are sometimes rusty.

6. The crowd cheered happily.

7. Miguel's brother is strong.

8. Wild horses galloped away.

9. The children were excited.

10. Some mountains are steep.

116. More Diagramming Practice

In a diagram compound sentence parts go on separate horizontal lines. A dashed line for the conjunction connects the compound parts.

SENTENCE: **Gloria and Chan sang and danced.**

To diagram a compound sentence, diagram each sentence separately, one above the other. Connect the sentences with a dashed line at the left of the sentences. Write the conjunction on the dashed line.

SENTENCE: **The sky was gray, and the wind blew hard.**

Diagram each of these sentences.

1. The cat and the dog slept peacefully.

2. My sister runs slowly but swims fast.

CONTINUED

Diagramming

3. That lemonade is cold and delicious.

4. The alarm rang loudly, and we marched outside.

5. The sun was hot, and Marcus walked slowly.

6. Tina waited calmly, but Janet was impatient.

Handbook of Terms

ABBREVIATIONS

An **abbreviation** is a short form of a word. An abbreviation often ends with a period.

- Abbreviations for words in addresses begin with capital letters and end with periods: Ave. = Avenue, Rd. = Road.

- Abbreviations for units of measure do not begin with capital letters: in. = inch, mi. = miles.

- Days of the week and most months of the year can be abbreviated. The abbreviations begin with capital letters and end with periods: Sat. = Saturday, Oct. = October.

- Titles and names can be abbreviated: Dr. M. S. Jones = Doctor Mary Scott Jones

- State postal abbreviations contain two capital letters and no period: IL, TX

ADJECTIVES

An **adjective** is a word that describes or points out a noun.

Articles point out nouns. *A, an,* and *the* are articles: *A* pear and *an* apple are in *the* blue bowl.

Demonstrative adjectives point out specific persons, places, or things.

- *This* and *that* point out one person, place, or thing.

- *These* and *those* point out more than one person, place, or thing.

- *This* and *these* point out persons, places, or things that are near.

- *That* and *those* point out persons, places, or things that are far.

Descriptive adjectives tell about size, shape, color, weight, age, or other features of nouns.

- A descriptive adjective can come before a noun: *sunny* morning, *hot* day.

- A descriptive adjective that comes after a being verb is a subject complement: The garden was *beautiful*.

- Some adjectives tell how many. They can tell exactly how many (*one, twelve, thirty*) or about how many (*several, few, many, some*).

Possessive adjectives show possession or ownership. A possessive adjective goes before a noun. The possessive adjectives are *my, your, his, her, its, our,* and *their: his* skateboard, *their* bikes.

Proper adjectives are adjectives that come from proper nouns. All other adjectives are called **common adjectives.** A proper adjective begins with a capital letter: *American* history.

See also **comparisons, sentences.**

ADVERBS

An **adverb** is a word that tells more about a verb.

- Some adverbs answer the question *when* or *how often:* It rained *yesterday.* We *usually* eat lunch at noon.

- Some adverbs answer the question *where:* Toshi bent his head *forward.* Sit *here* by the window.

- Some adverbs answer the question *how* or *in what manner:* Jason draws *well.* She dances the waltz *gracefully.*

A negative idea is expressed by using one negative word. This negative word may be *no, not, none, never,* or *nothing.* A sentence should contain only one negative word: I do not have *any* (not *no*) apples.

See also **comparisons.**

CAPITALIZATION

Many words begin with a capital letter, including the following:

- the first word of a sentence—The bell rang.

- names of people and pets—Did Harry name his owl Hedwig?

- names of streets, cities, states, and countries—Elm Street, Kansas City, Alabama, France

- days of the week and months of the year—Tuesday, June

- holidays—Christmas, Fourth of July

- an abbreviation if the word it stands for begins with a capital letter—Dec. = December, Mon. = Monday

- a title used before a person's name—Mr. Jones, Ms. Marlow

- the first word and the name of the person addressed in the salutation of a letter and the first word in the closing of a letter—Dear Marie, Yours truly,

- the first word, the last word, and each important word in the titles of books, plays, works of art, and poems—*Ramona the Brave, Starry Night,* "Keep a Poem in Your Pocket"

- the first word of a direct quotation—Mother said, "It's time for my favorite television program."

- proper adjectives—American flag, Dutch cocoa

Capital letters are also used for:

- the pronoun *I*

- two-letter state postal abbreviations—MA, NY, CA

- an initial (a capital letter followed by a period). A person may use an initial instead of a name—J. K. Rowling.

COMPARISONS

Many adjectives can be used to compare two or more persons, places, or things.

- To compare two persons, places, or things, add -er to most adjectives: *taller, cuter, hungrier, bigger.*

- To compare three or more persons, places, or things, add -est to most adjectives: *meanest, nicest, happiest, hottest.*

- If an adjective ends in e (*cute*), drop the final e and add -er or -est: *cuter, cutest.*

- If an adjective ends in y following a consonant (*lucky*), change the y to i and add -er or -est: *luckier, luckiest.*

- If a short adjective ends in a consonant that follows a vowel (*mad*), double the final consonant before adding -er or -est: *madder, maddest.*

- Some adjectives that compare are **irregular adjectives:** *good, better, best* and *bad, worse, worst.*

CONJUNCTIONS

A **conjunction** is a word used to connect words or groups of words.

A **coordinating conjunction** connects words or groups of words that are similar. The most common coordinating conjunctions are the words *and, but,* and *or:* Joshua *or* Leanne will cut out the words. Nancy drew *and* colored the pictures. Mika glued the words on the poster, *but* Carla glued the pictures.

CONTRACTIONS

A **contraction** is two words written as one word with one or more letters missing. An apostrophe (') is used to show where a letter or letters have been taken out. The word *not* is often part of a contraction: *aren't = are not, don't = do not, won't = will not.*

NOUNS

A **noun** is a word that names a person, a place, or a thing. A noun can be the subject of a sentence.

A **common noun** names any one member of a group of persons, places, or things: *queen, city, church.*

A **proper noun** names a particular person, place, or thing. A proper noun begins with a capital letter: *Queen Elizabeth, London, Westminster Abbey*

A **singular noun** names one person, place, or thing: *boy, ranch, berry.*

A **plural noun** names more than one person, place, or thing.

- To form the plural of a **regular noun,** add *-s* or *-es: boys, ranches.*

- If a regular singular noun ends in a consonant followed by *y* (*berry, fairy*), change the *y* to *i* and add *-es: berries, fairies.*

- If a regular singular noun ends in a vowel followed by *y* (*monkey*), add *-s: monkeys.*

- The plural of an **irregular noun** is not formed by adding *-s* or *-es: men, children, wolves, teeth, fish.*

A **collective noun** names a group of persons or things that are considered as a unit: The *band* played loudly.

A noun used in **direct address** names the person spoken to: *Carol,* would you help me?

A **possessive noun** expresses possession or ownership. The apostrophe (') is the sign of a possessive noun.

- To form the possessive of a singular noun, add *-'s* to the singular form: *architect's*

- To form the possessive of a plural noun that ends in *-s*, add an apostrophe to the plural form: *farmers'*

- To form the possessive of a plural noun that does not end in *-s*, add *-'s* to the plural form: *children's*

PRONOUNS

A **pronoun** is a word that takes the place of a noun or nouns. A **personal pronoun** has different forms.

A **plural** pronoun refers to more than one person, place, or thing. The plural pronouns are *we, us, ours, you, yours, they, them,* and *theirs.*

A **singular** pronoun refers to one person, place, or thing. The singular pronouns are *I, me, mine, you, yours, she, her, hers, he, him, his, it,* and *its.*

A **subject pronoun** may be used as the subject of a sentence. The subject pronouns are *I, you* (singular or plural), *he, she, it, we,* and *they: He* bought a new car. *You* look great, Carrie! *You* look great, boys!

- A compound subject may contain one or more subject pronouns. The subjects are connected by the word *and* or *or: He* and Margie are in the park. Joe and *she* are playing tennis. *He* or *she* will win the game.

An **object pronoun** may be used after the action verb in a sentence. The object pronouns are *me, you* (singular or plural), *him, her, it, us,* and *them:* I saw *her* at the mall. I saw *you* at the mall, Kevin. I saw *you* at the mall, girls.

A **possessive pronoun** shows possession or ownership. The possessive pronouns are *mine, yours, his, hers, its, ours,* and *theirs.* They never come before nouns. Although possessive pronouns show ownership, they do not contain apostrophes: The new skates are *hers.* That canoe is *ours.*

See also **sentences, subject-verb agreement.**

PUNCTUATION

Punctuation is used to make writing clearer.

An **apostrophe** (') is used as follows:

- to show ownership—the *cook's* hat, the *girls'* horses, the *children's* toys

- to replace letters left out in a contraction—*isn't* for *is not, don't* for *do not*

A **comma** (,) can be used in many ways, including the following:

- to separate words or groups of words in a series—We saw elephants, giraffes, hyenas, and monkeys.

- to set off parts of addresses—321 Spring Rd., Apt. 4

- to separate a city and a state—Atlanta, Georgia

- to set off parts of dates—June 12, 2010

- to set off words in direct address—Josie, I'm so pleased that you called me this morning.

- to set off a direct quotation—
  "We have only vanilla and chocolate today," he explained.

- to separate simple sentences connected by the conjunctions *and, but,* and *or*—She called his name, but he didn't answer her.

- after the salutation in a friendly letter and the closing in all letters—Dear Ben, Sincerely yours,

An **exclamation point** (!) is used at the end of an exclamation: What a celebration that was!

A **period** (.) is used in these ways:

- at the end of a telling sentence—His dog ran away.

- at the end of a command—Please find him.

- after many abbreviations—Dr. = Doctor, ft. = feet.

A **question mark** (?) is used at the end of a question: What time is it*?*

Quotation marks (" ") are used as follows:

- before and after every direct quotation—
  "Let's go shopping," said Michiko.
  Father said, "I haven't eaten lunch."

- to enclose titles of poems—"What I Left Where"

SENTENCES

A **sentence** is a group of words that expresses a complete thought. A sentence has a subject and a predicate.

The **subject** names who or what a sentence is about.

- The **simple subject** is a noun or pronoun: The *man* is riding his bike.

- The **complete subject** is the simple subject and all the words that go with it: *The tall young man* is riding his bike.

- A subject pronoun may be used as the subject of a sentence: *We* went to the mall.

- If a sentence has more than one simple subject, it has a **compound subject:** *Ivan* and *John* argued with the grocer.

The **predicate** tells something about the subject.

- The **simple predicate** is a verb or verb phrase: Teresa *waved.*

- The **complete predicate** is the verb and all the words that go with it: Teresa *waved from the window.*

- If a sentence has more than one simple predicate, it has a **compound predicate:** Our hamster *eats* and *exercises* at night.

A **subject complement** can follow a being verb. A subject complement is an adjective that describes the subject: The boy was *angry.*

A **compound sentence** contains two short sentences that are related to each other. They are combined with a comma, followed by the word *and, but,* or *or.* We went to the park, *and* we played softball. It started to rain, *but* we kept playing.

A **command** tells what to do. It is usually ends with a period: Go to the store. Please pick up the papers.

An **exclamation** expresses strong or sudden emotion. It ends with an exclamation point: What a loud noise that was!

A **question** is an asking sentence. It ends with a question mark and often starts with a question word: Where is my pen?

A **run-on sentence** is a sentence in which two sentences are combined incorrectly: We will play checkers, we will watch a movie. To correct a run-on sentence, add the word *and, but,* or *or* after the comma. When a run-on sentence is corrected, it becomes a compound sentence: We will play checkers, *or* we will watch a movie.

A **statement** is a telling sentence. It ends with a period: The sun is shining.

SUBJECT-VERB AGREEMENT

A subject and its verb must agree.

- In the simple present tense, singular nouns and the singular pronouns *he, she,* and *it* take verbs that end in *-s* or *-es:* The boy *runs.* He *runs.*

- In the simple present tense, plural nouns, plural subject pronouns (*we, you, they*), and the subject pronouns *I* and *you* take verbs that do not end in *-s* or *-es:* Horses *run.* We *run.* You *run.* They *run.* I *run.*

- Use *am* or *was* with the subject pronoun *I:* I *am* a soccer player. I *was* late for practice.

- Use *is* or *was* with a singular noun or the subject pronouns *he, she,* and *it:* Paris *is* a city. She *was* a pianist.

- Use *are* or *were* with a plural noun or the subject pronouns *you, we,* and *they:* Dogs *are* good pets. You *are* the winner. You *are* all winners. We *were* happy. They *were* my neighbors.

TENSE

The tense of a verb shows when its action happens.

- The **simple present tense** tells about something that is always true or about an action that happens again and again: The sun *rises* in the east. I *play* the piano every afternoon.

- The **simple past tense** tells about an action that happened in the past. The simple past of a regular verb is formed by adding *-d* or *-ed*: I *played* the piano yesterday afternoon. The simple past of an irregular verb is not formed by adding *-d* or *-ed:* I *sang.* They *wrote.* She *sat.*

- The **future tense** tells about an action that will happen in the future. The future tense can be formed in two ways. One way is to use the helping verb *will* and the present part of a verb: They *will visit* the museum on Sunday.

- Another way to form the future tense is to use *am going to, is going to,* or *are going to* with the present part of the verb: I *am going to play* shortstop.

- The **present progressive tense** tells what is happening now. The present progressive tense is formed with *am, is,* or *are* and the present participle: He *is eating* his lunch now.

- The **past progressive tense** tells what was happening in the past. The past progressive tense is formed with *was* or *were* and the present participle: He *was eating* his lunch when I saw him.

See also **subject-verb agreement, verbs.**

VERBS

An **action verb** is a word tells what someone or something does: Jake *sings.* The dog *barked.*

A **being verb** shows what someone or something is. Being verbs do not express action. Sometimes a being verb is used to join the subject of a sentence to an adjective: He *is* happy. The bag *was* heavy.

A **helping verb** is a verb that is always followed by a main verb. Some helping verbs are *am, is, are, was, were, be, being, been, shall, will, may, can, has, have, had, do, does, did, should, would, could,* and *must:* Mom *is washing* the dishes. I *will help* her.

A verb has four **principal parts:** the **present**, the **present participle**, the **past**, and the **past participle**.

- The present participle is formed by adding *-ing* to the present: *jumping, writing, hopping.* The present participle is used with a form of the helping verb *be:* I *am jumping.* She *was writing.* They *are hopping.*

- The past and the past participle of **regular verbs** are formed by adding *-d* or *-ed* to the present: *jump, jumped.* The past participle is used with a form of the helping verb *have:* I *have jumped.* She *has written.* They *had hopped.*

- The past and the past participle of **irregular verbs** are not formed by adding *-ed* to the present: *sang, sung.*

See also **subject-verb agreement, tense.**